INSIGHT GUIDES

BRUGES

StepbyStep

APA PUBLICATIONS

Part of the Langenscheidt Publishing Group

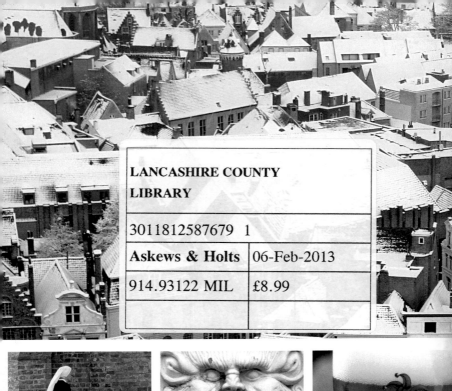

CONTENTS

Above: Dijver canal; mussels by the Burg; detail from the tombs in the Church of Our Lady; Beguinage; literary Damme, a pleasant stroll from Bruges.

ABOUT THIS BOOK

This *Step by Step Guide* has been produced by the editors of Insight Guides, whose books have set the standard for visual travel guides since 1970. With top-quality photography and authoritative recommendations, this guidebook brings you the very best of Bruges in a series of 15 tailor-made tours.

WALKS AND TOURS

The tours in the book provide something to suit all budgets, tastes and trip lengths. As well as covering Bruges's many classic attractions, the routes track lesser-known sights, and there are also excursions for those who want to extend their visit outside the city. The tours embrace a range of interests, so whether you are an art fan, a gourmet, a history buff or have kids to entertain, you will find an option to suit.

We recommend reading the whole of a tour before setting out. This should help you to familiarise yourself with the route and enable you to plan where to stop for refreshments – options are shown in the 'Food and Drink' boxes, recognisable by the knife-and-fork sign, on most pages.

For our pick of the walks by theme, consult Recommended Tours For… *(see pp.6–7)*.

OVERVIEW

The tours are set in context by this introductory section, giving an overview of the city to set the scene, plus background information on food and drink, shopping and entertainment. A succinct history timeline highlights the key events that have shaped Bruges over the centuries.

DIRECTORY

Also supporting the tours is a Directory chapter, with a clearly organised A–Z of practical information, our pick of where to stay while you are in the city and select restaurant listings; these eateries complement the more low-key cafés and restaurants that feature within the tours and are intended to offer a wider choice for evening dining. Also included here are some nightlife listings.

The Author

Katharine Mill lived in Belgium for a decade until 2008. Based in Brussels, she was lifestyle editor and then deputy editor of *The Bulletin*, a weekly English-language magazine, covering subjects ranging from politics and fashion to contemporary dance. Initially resistant to the charm of Bruges, she became a convert following exposure to the paintings of Jan van Eyck, a springtime walk through the Beguinage and a summer evening's cycle along the canal from Gouden Handrei to Speelmansrei. This is her third book on Bruges for Insight Guides.

Nicholas Hirst lives in Brussels and also writes for *The Bulletin*. In 2008 he spent a year in Bruges as a researcher and now visits the city regularly for work and pleasure.

Margin Tips
Shopping tips, historical facts, handy hints and useful information on activities help visitors to make the most of their time in Bruges.

Feature Boxes
Notable topics are highlighted in these special boxes.

Key Facts Box
This box gives details of the distance covered on the tour, plus an estimate of how long it should take. It also states where the route starts and finishes, and gives key travel information such as which days are best to do the route or handy transport tips.

Footers
Look here for the tour name, a map reference and the main attraction on the double-page.

Food and Drink
Recommendations of where to stop for refreshment are given in these boxes. The numbers prior to each restaurant/café name link to references in the main text. Restaurants in the Food and Drink boxes are plotted on the maps.

The € signs at the end of each entry reflect the approximate cost of a two-course meal for one, with a glass of house wine. These should be seen as a guide only. Price ranges, also quoted on the inside back flap for easy reference, are:

€€€€	over 100 euros
€€€	60–100 euros
€€	30–60 euros
€	below 30 euros

Route Map
Detailed cartography shows the tour clearly plotted with numbered dots. For more detailed mapping, see the pull-out map slotted inside the back cover.

ART ENTHUSIASTS

Flemish Primitives, Bosch and
the Symbolists vie for attention at
the Groeninge (walk 4), Hans
Memling has the monopoly in
St John's Hospital (walk 5), while
one masterpiece – the van Eyck
altarpiece in St Bavo's – justifies
the trip to Ghent (walk 15).

RECOMMENDED TOURS FOR...

ESCAPING THE CROWDS

Follow the lapping waters of the Langerei to the
charming museum of Our Lady of the Pottery church
(walk 9), wander the district west of 't Zand (walk 11)
or cycle up the canal to peaceful Damme (walk 12).

CHILDREN

Wander along canals past fishermen
and houseboats on the way to the
Astrid Park (walk 7), visit the adorable
Folklore Museum (walk 6) or take to
the beach at Ostend (walk 13).

FOOD AND DRINK

Chocoholics will get a tasty treat at Choco-Story
(walk 3), while beer-lovers should sample the only
beer still brewed in Bruges at the Half Moon Brewery
(walk 5). For seafood, nothing beats Ostend (walk 13).

SPORTY TYPES

Climb the 366 steps of the Belfry tower
(walk 2), cycle or walk to Damme along
the canal that Napoleon dug (walk 12), or
venture to Ostend for a bracing dip in the
North Sea and a pedal-buggy ride along
the prom (walk 13).

GREEN SPACES

Discover a real secret garden, the Hof Sebrechts Park (walk 10), enjoy a picnic in the shade at tranquil Astrid Park (walk 7) or explore a village surrounded by green fields and polder in Damme (walk 12).

HISTORIANS

Stalk the haunts of medieval merchants (walk 8), inspect the crusader's trophy that inspires religious devotion at the Holy Blood Basilica (walk 3) or revisit the tragedy of World War I in the cemeteries and battlefields around Ypres (tour 14).

ROMANTIC BRUGES

Watch swans glide over the mirror-like Minnewater, or 'Lake of Love' (walk 5), or set out early to enjoy uninterrupted views from the Rozenhoedkaai and along leafy Groenerei (walk 7).

RAINY DAYS

Situated side by side, the Groeninge, Arentshuis and Gruuthuse museums are ideal for an indoor day (walk 4), or travel to Ypres, for the excellent In Flanders Fields Museum and Sanctuary Wood (tour 14).

FILM BUFFS

Follow in the steps of the hitman duo from *In Bruges*: dine at Cafedraal (walk 2) and discuss the Holy Blood at the Jerusalem Church (walk 6). But try to avoid a denouement with your boss in the Belfry (walk 2).

OVERVIEW

An overview of Bruges's geography, customs and culture, plus illuminating background information on food and drink, shopping, entertainment and history.

CITY INTRODUCTION

Medieval Bruges is one of the most romantic destinations in Europe. Glassy green canals meander around gabled almshouses, Gothic churches, world-class art galleries and boutique hotels, all packaged in an egg-shaped central district less than 2km (1¼ miles) across.

Printing Pioneers
The first printed book in English was produced in Bruges in 1473 by William Caxton for Margaret, duchess of Burgundy and sister of English kings Edward IV and Richard III.

Bruges – Brugge to its residents – is a provincial town that hit the big time with its cloth trade in the Middle Ages, riding high for 400 years before sinking into oblivion, cut off from the world. Centuries on, 19th-century heritage enthusiasts chanced upon the time-capsule city and shook it from its Sleeping Beauty slumber, restoring it to a splendour that celebrates the Gothic and Baroque, Renaissance and modern.

The city may live off its past but it is not content to reside there. A startlingly modern music venue, incessant property renovation, chic new restaurants and a lively programme of contemporary dance, experimental music and film disprove accusations that it is little more than a museum piece. Yes, tourism dominates the city, but it is fantastically easy to escape the crowds.

GEOGRAPHY

This city of 20,000 people is located 11km (7 miles) from the North Sea coast and is the capital of West Flanders, a province that contains the entire 67km (42 miles) of Belgium's coastline and is bordered by France, the Netherlands and the provinces of Hainaut (in French-speaking Wallonia) and East Flanders.

With the reclaimed polders of the maritime plain to the north and west, and sandy pastoral land to the east and south, the municipality of Bruges includes three distinct areas: the historic centre (a Unesco World Heritage Site), contained by a 7km- (4⅓-mile) long ring canal along the line of the former city walls; the suburbs, named after historic parishes situated outside the walls: Sint-Michiels, Sint-Andries, Sint-Jozef and so on; and a tongue of land stretching north to the sea, including the village of Lissewege and the port of Zeebrugge.

As long as you are within the centre, and there is little reason to venture outside, the only sensible means of getting around is on foot or by bike.

HISTORY

The city grew up from a Gallo-Roman settlement, Bruggia, first mentioned in AD851. It rose to prominence as a cloth town and trading hub, its weavers

renowned for their skill in transforming English wool into the finest tapestries and garments in Europe.

Fortunes waxed and waned with time and tides. Fierce coastal storms opened and closed the city's access to the sea starting in the 11th century, when silting prevented ships from sailing directly into the centre. A flood in 1134 created a new sea route from the Zwin inlet to Damme, 7km (4⅓ miles) to the northeast. Bruges made Damme its outer port, and dug canals to ferry goods to and from the city on small barges.

Golden Age

From 1200–1400, the city was an important member of the Hanseatic League, a network of trading cities across Europe. Foreign merchants built grand consulates and settled here, trading metals, fur and wine for locally produced cloth. The city saw the birth of the world's first stock exchange, and became a cultish place of pilgrimage, inspired by a supposed relic of Christ's blood brought back from the Crusades (and still presented for veneration in a basilica built for the purpose). The Gothic City Hall and many churches and mansions survive from this period.

Wealth and religious devotion promoted a flourishing artistic community: painters Jan van Eyck and Hans Memling made Bruges their home, catering to the court of the dukes of Burgundy, successors to the counts of Flanders and great patrons of the arts. Their rule was renowned as a period of refinement and festivities: banquets, tournaments and processions helped local craftsmen diversify into illuminated manuscripts, lace and other luxury items.

Decline

Protracted conflicts between the royal houses of England and France eventually took their toll on a city ruled by the French yet dependent on English wool. Disputes between the citizens and their rulers were compounded by the silting up of the sea-channel. By the early 16th century, Bruges was effectively cut off from the world. Courtiers and merchants abandoned the town, while religious wars and persecution forced many skilled craftsmen to flee.

Above from far left: the Procession of the Holy Blood occurs every year on Ascension Day *(see p.38)*; Bruges rooftops and stepped gables.

Left: the Belfry is one of the three towers that dominate the city skyline.

Disaster then has brought riches today, as centuries of decline left many historic monuments untouched. By the mid-18th century, the much-dwindled population survived by making lace, a cottage industry that was eventually decimated by industrialisation.

Modern Era

Belgian independence and the arrival of the railway brought early tourists travelling from Ostend to Brussels – many of them English people en route to the Waterloo battlefield – who came across this time-warped city. A heritage movement was launched, Gothic buildings and historic monuments were repaired, and the tourist industry took off.

CLIMATE

Bruges has the warm summers and mild winters typical of a maritime temperate climate. Snow is rare, but rain is common. July and August are the warmest months, with an average maximum of 22°C (72°F), and temperatures hovering around 30°C (86°F) on the hottest days. June is sunniest. The coldest months are December to February, when daily averages hover at 1-5°C (34–41°F). On the chilliest days, bitter winds from the north and east can sweep across the flat polder landscape of Flanders, and make the damp air seem colder still.

POLITICS AND ECONOMICS

Bruges is the capital of West Flanders, one of 11 provinces in Belgium, a constitutional monarchy with a federal parliamentary system. The king is the head of state, while the prime minister is the head of government, leading a multi-party coalition of ministers, half of whom represent each of the Flemish and the French-speaking communities.

The main political families split in the 1970s into separate parties aligned along linguistic grounds: in Flanders, the right-wing Liberals are represented by the VLD, the socially conservative Christian Democrats by the CD&V and the Socialists by the SP.A. There is also a Green Party and a strong nationalist and far-right movement. Coalitions are very much the norm, with both the mayor of Bruges, Christian Democrat Patrick Moenaert, and the federal prime minister, Socialist Elio di Rupo, heading broad political coalitions.

Flemish Autonomy

Flanders has enjoyed a degree of autonomy ever since Charlemagne divided his kingdom in AD843 and created the County of Flanders. The wealthy medieval cities won their own charters and liberties, despite often bitter dispute with the French-speaking aristocracy. After living under French, Habsburg, Spanish and Dutch rule, independence in 1830 crowned Leopold of Saxe-

Coburg-Gotha as king of the Belgians, reaffirming French as the language of power, even though 60 percent of the population spoke Flemish. To get on in the army, public administration, universities and the law, the Flemish were until recently obliged to speak French *(see margin, right)*.

In the 19th century, Wallonia grew rich on its coal resources, while Flanders remained largely agricultural. A militant literary movement hailed by Bruges poet-priest Guido Gezelle, helped the Dutch language achieve parity with French in public administration in 1898.

Flemish nationalism reemerged in World War I, when it was exposed that 75 percent of frontline troops were Dutch-speaking and could not understand their officers, 75 percent of whom could not speak Dutch. Thousands died as a result; some Flemings sided with the German occupiers in protest. The Nazis exploited Flemish dissatisfaction in World War II, and won the support of numerous collaborators.

Devolution

A reversal of economic fortunes has led Flanders to achieve greater autonomy. Decline of the coal and steel industries in the south has been countered by growth in the high-tech and port-services sectors in the north. Progressive devolution since the 1970s has given the regions control over economic, social and cultural policy, while tax and foreign policy remain federal competences.

There is great resentment in Flanders that the thriving local economy is hampered by 'financial transfers' to the south, where former industrial towns are blighted by unemployment. But as any major reform must be passed by at least 50 percent of French-speakers, the minority community is effectively able to prevent change, a situation criticised as undemocratic by many in Flanders. In recent elections, the far-right Vlaams Belang (Flemish Interest) party has won one in four votes across Flanders, forcing the mainstream parties to form ever wider coalitions and adapt their own policies to demand further devolution.

PEOPLE

Despite political tensions, most Flemings muddle along happily with their compatriots in day-to-day life. As Belgians they share much common ground: strong family values, a respect for convention and love of material comforts, not to mention a good meal with beer. As many French-speakers as Flemings holiday on the Flemish coast, while many Flemings retire to the Ardennes.

Bruges has none of the students that give Antwerp, Ghent and Brussels their edge, while the Moroccan and Turkish communities that are so visible in other cities are all but absent here. The cultured, slightly older-than-average locals are very polite to the millions of visitors who pass through Bruges, but keep a distance with all but their closest circle.

Flemish and Dutch

One reason for the late recognition of Flemish in public life is that there was no standardised form of the language. Flemings speak a variety of dialects and cannot always understand people from another region (the West Flemish dialect spoken around Bruges is famously difficult to understand). Although loosely called a language, Flemish *(vlaams)* is strictly a collection of dialects that are a variation of Dutch *(nederlands)*, now the lingua franca and official language. It differs somewhat in pronunciation and about 2,000 words of vocabulary from the language spoken in the Netherlands, but is monitored, along with the Dutch spoken in Surinam, by the Dutch Language Council.

FOOD AND DRINK

The Belgians are famous for their mussels, beer, chocolate and fries, but how about North Sea shrimps and Ostend sole, Mechelen white asparagus, 'Belgian Blue' beef and wild boar? It's a well-used phrase but as true today as ever: everyone eats well in Belgium.

Above: seasonal game dishes.

A tradition of medieval banquets and Brueghelian feasts has left its mark on the Belgians, who love nothing better than a hearty, convivial meal with family or friends. Large family groups get together on Sundays and public holidays for a long, lazy lunch stretching far into the afternoon.

Large numbers of tourists mean that eating out in Bruges is more expensive than in other cities, and the high turnover of clientele means that restaurants in prime locations need not fear for their reputation. In addition, with no major student population, there is little demand for dining on a shoestring, so budget options are few and far between.

LOCAL CUISINE

In Flanders, the regional cuisine is dominated by fish and seafood, grilled meats and fresh seasonal vegetables. Brussels is famous for its *stoemp* (mash with vegetables, served with sausage) and meatballs in tomato sauce, while Wallonia has excellent mushrooms, game and wild boar from the Ardennes, cooked in

rich, fruity sauces enhanced with beer. Mussels, the nation's favourite food, are in fact imported mostly from the Netherlands. And of course, everyone eats fries.

Typical dishes include a dark beef stew cooked for hours with beer (*Vlaamse stoofkarbonaden/carbonades flamandes*) and *waterzooi*, a Ghent stew of fish or chicken, potatoes, carrots and onion in a thin, creamy sauce. In season from August to April, mussels (*mosselen*) are cooked in a thin stock of celery and onion and served in a large black pot – use an empty shell as a pincer for eating the rest – accompanied by fries and mayonnaise. Game dishes are mainly available in autumn and winter, while Belgian endive wrapped in ham and baked in a white sauce topped with cheese (*gegratineerd witloof*) is another warming winter dish. Shrimp croquettes, a starter of tiny shrimps mixed with béchamel sauce and deep-fried in breadcrumbs, served with a sprig of deep-fried parsley, is a year-round favourite. And every chef has his own recipe for eel in green sauce (*paling in't groen*), a light dish where

the eel is cooked with a herby mixture of chervil, spinach, parsley, sorrel and tarragon and lemon balm.

Few Belgians are vegetarians, so visiting veggies should avoid Belgian cuisine or they may find themselves stuck with omelettes and vegetable side dishes. Lebanese, Oriental, Indian and some Italian restaurants will offer many tastier options.

WHERE TO EAT

Restaurants

Everyone in Belgium dines out, and there are restaurants to suit all tastes. Neighbourhood establishments – many serving international cuisine such as Greek, Lebanese or Italian – will have paper tablecloths and toothpicks in a plastic pot; the formal variety will serve artful creations inspired by French cuisine, and have a dedicated wine waiter. Chain restaurants are unheard of beyond fast-food outlets; the majority are characterful family-run firms that take pride in serving well-presented, good food. Staff are likely to have followed professional training and can advise on dishes and wines.

Many of the high-end establishments are owned by chefs who have made their name working in the best kitchens in the business, and established enough credibility to stamp their personality on a solo venture, designing a unique menu style. Since the country is so small – and Flanders and Wallonia almost separate countries within themselves – reputations and career history are widely known and discussed by food critics, prompting locals to travel a fair distance for a good restaurant. They are mainly open from noon–2 or 2.30pm and 6.30–10pm.

Brasseries

There is no exact definition for the title, but for our purposes brasseries are open all day for drinks and prioritise tables for diners around mealtimes. Less formal and more lively than a restaurant, they will serve a full, predictable menu of North Sea fish dishes, salads, steaks and classics like Belgian beef stew, chicory *gratin* and rabbit cooked in cherry beer, plus a standard selection of desserts: chocolate mousse, tarte Tatin, crème brûlée and ices. The large majority of tourist-focused restaurants in Bruges are brasseries; several will also serve food outside standard mealtimes (but if they say 'The kitchen is closed,' you will get a microwaved dish).

Bars and Cafés

Many bars do basic menus, such as soup, spaghetti Bolognese, omelettes and toasted sandwiches. The cuisine is not fantastic, but is perfectly satisfying for empty bellies *(see margin tip, p.17)*.

Above from far left: hearty Flemish fare; mussels are served in a large black pot with fries; flavoured Belgian gin; tucking into a stew.

Booking Advisable
The restaurants in Bruges are busy year-round and not just in peak seasons. It is therefore advisable to book for evening meals in advance, otherwise you might struggle to find a table on the night. Most will be happy to speak English if you call in advance to reserve a table.

Tearooms

Tearooms are a feature of the coast and in Bruges; they are uncommon elsewhere in the country. Targeted squarely at day-trippers, they serve light lunches and afternoon snacks such as waffles, pancakes and ices, mainly with hot or soft drinks, although many also serve alcohol. In Bruges, they also offer a good-value alternative to hotel breakfast, if this is not included in your room price.

Fries Van

The fries van *(frietkot)* – usually a fixed caravan – is an institution in every Belgian town; perfect for a budget munch on the go, and no calories spared. In Bruges, the *frietkot* has pride of place on the Markt, in front of the Belfry.

Chips are cut thick and fried twice for the unique Belgian consistency – an initial long fry to cook the potato, then a rest, then a hotter flash-fry for the crunchy edge – and served with salt added, wrapped in a paper cornet or on a plastic tray *(bak)*. The server will ask if you want them open – the classic way, to eat standing up by the van – or to take away *(Om mee te nemen)*, wrapped in paper.

Sauces cost about 50 cents extra and include mayonnaise, tartare, ketchup, curry-ketchup, spicy mayo mixes Samourai and Andalousian, and red-hot Pili Pili. You can ask to have the sauce on the side, in a mini plastic tray, for dipping. The vans also sell soft drinks and a variety of meat accompaniments: meatball *(bal)*, meat stick *(fricandel)*, burger, brochette (wooden skewer with meat and veg). For the max-out meal, go for a *mitraillette* (literally, machine-gun): a long baguette roll filled with a brochette, salad and fries, and lathered with sauce.

DRINKS

Beer

Belgium produces around 500 types of beer, and each brand must be served in its own distinctive glass. There used to be thousands of local breweries – just one survives in Bruges – but few could compete with the Leuven-based brewer of Stella Artois, Hoegaarden, Leffe and Jupiler. With roots that can be traced back to 1366, it is now the world's no. 1 brewer, renamed AB InBev following a merger with Anheuser-Busch in late 2008.

Beer is served chilled from the tap or the bottle. Typical local varieties include the following:

Lambic beers are wild beers, exposed to wild yeast during fermentation. Gueuze is one type of lambic, which are often quite sour and dry and to which fruit flavours are often added. Kriek is a lambic beer fermented with Morello cherries, giving it its characteristic dark-red hue.

Trappist beers are brewed in an abbey under the control of Trappist monks and are top-fermented ales. Of 171 Trappist monasteries in the world, seven produce beer, six of them in Belgium: Chimay, Orval, Rochefort, Westmalle, Westvleteren and Achelse Kruis.

White beer *(witbier)* is cloudy and often comes with a slice of lemon. Hoegaarden and Brugse Tarwebier are two varieties.

Genever

Belgian gin, increasingly hard to find, is made from distilled grains (usually barley, which gives it more body than English gin), flavoured with juniper berries, caraway seeds or fennel. This was the tipple that 17th-century British troops discovered during the Dutch War of Independence against the Spanish, giving them 'Dutch courage'. It comes in three varieties: Oude, the old, straw-coloured, pungently sweet version; Jonge, a younger, more delicately flavoured variety; and Korenwijn, which is cask-aged with a high percentage of malted spirit.

Mineral Water

The hilly Ardennes in southern Belgium has several mineral-water sources. Many of these are bottled for sale, including Spa, Chaudfontaine and Bru. Tap water is perfectly drinkable, but few restaurants will be happy to serve it with a meal.

Tea and Coffee

Tea in Belgium is invariably insipid, served as a cup of hot (not boiling) water with a flavourless bag on the side. Fruit-flavoured and herbal teas are widely available, however, and commonly drunk at the end of a meal in the evening. Fresh mint tea, inspired by the Moroccan community, may be available in trendy places. Coffee is better: standard coffee

(koffie) comes in a medium-sized cup and saucer with a dose of creamer on the side; milky coffee *(koffie verkeerd)* is usually a glass with a dose of espresso and hot milk. Cappuccino is usually made with a dollop of sweet, whipped cream on a black coffee and not frothy milk. Large coffee chains ubiquitous elsewhere that serve vats of milky coffee have not yet reached Belgium, with, for example, barely a handful of Starbucks in the country.

Café Nibbles
Most cafés serve a complimentary nibble when you buy a round of drinks: a sweet biscuit with a hot drink, peanuts with cold drinks. In addition, many also offer a 'mixed portion' for a few euros – a plate of cheese or salami chunks, served with mustard, pickles and celery salt. Shared between 2–4 people these make for a filling snack with a few beers.

Left: Ghent-based Dulle Griet's Kwak beer comes in a 1.5-litre glass.

SHOPPING

Few visitors leave Bruges without a consignment of chocolate and beer, two products for which Belgium is rightly famed. Other souvenirs may include lace, art books and prints, or hip fashions from a world-renowned designer.

Opening Times

Store opening hours in Belgium are generally 9.30/10am to 6/6.30pm. As many businesses are family firms, it is common to see extended closures in summer, most commonly from 21 July (the Belgian national holiday) to 15 August (Assumption, also a public holiday). Few stores except those aimed at tourists open on Sundays.

Gift-Wrapping

Most stores will gift-wrap your purchase at no extra charge, so make sure to indicate if you are buying something as a present. This is a fabulous service, as sales staff are typically very skilled at making gifts look luxurious. At especially busy times, you may need to be patient.

Lace, beer and chocolate shops are concentrated in the well-worn groove between the Burg, Markt and Beguinage, along Breidelstraat, Wollestraat, Katelijnestraat and around Walplein. Needless to say, you will not find the best bargains in these areas.

Elsewhere, the main shopping areas are the parallel streets running west from the Markt to the 't Zand: Steenstraat and Geldmuntstraat (which become Zuidzandstraat and Noordzandstraat). Around St Saviour's Cathedral are some good antique stores, while Wollestraat, Sint-Jakobsstraat and Vlamingstraat have stylish interiors stores.

BEER

Bruges has a number of specialist beer shops, all within easy walking distance of the Markt. These shops are ideal for insider recommendations, hard-to-find varieties and souvenir packs with glasses. Three of the best are: Bacchus Cornelius at Academiestraat 17; The Bottle Shop at Wollestraat 13, and De Bier Tempel at Philipstockstraat 7.

If you simply want Leffe, Duvel or Chimay, you will get a better price in a supermarket: Carrefour Express (Zuid-zandstraat 5, Katelijnestraat 76, Langerei 17 and Vlamingstraat 2) or Proxy Delhaize (Noordzandstraat 4). If you are driving back to the UK, do not count on buying Belgian beer in the Calais hypermarkets, which mainly stock French pils.

CHOCOLATE

Belgium makes some of the best chocolate in the world – made exclusively with cocoa butter – and is most famous for its pralines: sculpted shells containing various fillings, of which a dizzying variety exist. Every Belgian has their own opinion on who makes the best, and on Saturday afternoons you can see people lining up at chocolatiers to buy a box of mixed pralines, which can be chosen according to preference (no dark; all dark; no alcohol, etc). A box *(ballotin)* of pralines is a common gift to your hosts when you are invited to dinner.

The large chains are reliable and good and are all on Steenstraat: Leonidas (cheapest), Neuhaus, Galler and Godiva. Local makers are numerous, but select wisely: Van Oost (Wollestraat 11), Sweertvaegher (Philipstockstraat 29) and Chocolate Line (Simon Stevinplein 17) are all authentic.

LACE

Once the main local export, lace is still widely promoted in the city. Most items on sale are machine-made in the Far East, but handmade lace, including antique samples, can still be found; most shops sell a mix of the two – and none is correct to claim that they are the only one selling the handmade variety.

Handmade lace is expensive: for a large tablecloth or long wedding veil, count on paying upwards of 400 euros. The shop near the Lace Centre in St Anna, 't Apostelientje (Balstraat 11), is very good, as are Irma (Oude Burg 4), Kantuweeltje (Philipstockstraat 11) and Claeys Antique (Katelijnestraat 54).

BOOKS, MUSIC AND ART

Comic strips are Belgium's biggest literary export. De Striep Club at Katelijnestraat 42 is the best address in Bruges for comics, though most bookstores boast a healthy selection of Tintin books and other local comic stars.

The Markt is good for general books, international press, music and multimedia, with several bookstores and the large FNAC department store. Just off the square at Sint-Jakobsstraat 7 is Raaklijn, a favourite among book-lovers.

Its musical counterpart, selling a rarefied selection from jazz to Flemish folk, is Rombaux (Mallebergplaats 13). It isn't cheap, but there are listening rooms and the staff are very knowledgeable.

Another excellent source of books and gift ideas is the museum shop of the Groeninge Museum, which is separate from the museum in the courtyard of the Arentshuis. It stocks books, cards and posters of works by Flemish Primitives and other Belgian artists, but also art-themed jewellery, watches and bags.

FASHION AND DESIGN

Belgium's fashion design roster is impressive: Ann Demeulemeester, Dries van Noten, Diane von Furstenberg, Martin Margiela and Olivier Theyskens are just some home-grown fashion darlings. Young, Bruges-born Bruno Pieters has been tipped for the top by Suzy Menkes. At the time of writing, his new label is only available online (www.honestby.com), though cutting-edge Belgian fashion can be admired at L'Héroïne (Noordzandstraat 32), Essentiel (Noordzandstraat 42) and Olivier Strelli (Eiermarkt 3 for women, Geldmuntstraat 19 for men).

For accessories, Optique Hoet at Vlamingstraat 19 is a local, avant-garde glasses designer that also does high-end furniture. And Delvaux (Breidelstraat 2) is an established Brussels leather goods firm, which does luxurious and classic handbags, gloves, scarves and jewellery.

Two rustic and romantic homestyle stores also deserve a mention: the Dutch chain Dille & Kamille on Simon Stevinplein 17–18, and adorably romantic Ark van Zarren at Zuidzandstraat 19.

Above from far left: luxurious leather goods at Delvaux; delicious chocolate truffles; Belgian beer; handmade lace.

Sales
Sales periods in Belgium are strictly regulated and take place in the months of January and July only. Look out for the magic words *Solden* (Sales) or *Total Uitverkoop* (Everything Must Go). Mark-downs tend to increase during the course of the month, starting at 30 percent and increasing to 70 percent.

ENTERTAINMENT

Bruges has developed into a major player on the Flemish arts scene, with a renowned resident orchestra and a calendar rich in festivals covering jazz, early music, world film and dance. Its nightlife is eclectic and unpretentious, ideal for relaxing after a hard day pounding the cobbles.

Rather like the city itself, Bruges's cultural scene is small but perfectly formed. The new Concert Hall, historic City Theatre and laid-back festivals attract world-class orchestras, cutting-edge dance companies, experimental music composers and famed jazz artists. The nightlife scene is more restrained, but contains a great selection for somewhere so easy to explore on foot, making the transition easy from cosy beer bar to mini dance club – and not an entrance charge or stroppy doorman in sight.

MUSIC

Classical

Bruges has a strong reputation on the classical music scene, upheld by the large number of concerts held in churches around in the city and the state-of-the-art Concert Hall (Concertgebouw). Large orchestras perform in the 1,300-seat auditorium, while the 300-seat chamber music room – an architectural showpiece with concrete vertical tiers – is ideal for intimate performances.

Fans of early music are especially well served. The Concert Hall's resident orchestra is period-instrument ensemble Anima Eterna, led by renowned harpischordist-pianist-conductor Jos van Immerseel. And the Bruges leg of the Flanders Festival, held each year in late July–early August, is famous for its Musica Antiqua programme, which celebrates modern versions of early music.

Carillon

Wherever you go in Bruges, you are rarely beyond earshot of the 17th-century carillon in the city's Belfry, which is programmed to play a variety of tunes, from Mozart to Jacques Brel, every 15 minutes. The city's carilloneur also performs live concerts which last 45 minutes; these can best be heard from the courtyard of the Cloth Hall.

Contemporary, Rock and Jazz

The country-wide Ars Musica festival in March and April is a contemporary music bonanza, with several concerts in Bruges, while the Concert Hall programme includes regular avant-garde classical, electronica and jazz events, some of which are showcased at the Come On! Festival in February.

The local jazz and rock scene is small-scale compared to bigger cities, but still

Tickets
Tickets for concerts, gigs and other performances are sold at the In&Uit tourist office and box office on 't Zand (daily 10am–6pm). For an advance overview of what's on, the West Flanders cultural events website www.tinck.be is easy to navigate even without speaking Dutch: choose the relevant date and select 'Brugge' as the municipality *(gemeente)*.

manages to attract international artists for intimate gigs. Located just outside the historic centre, the Cactus Musiekcentrum, based primarily in the MaZ venue just west of the station, features upcoming indie bands as well as established figures on the world and folk circuit. It also organises the summertime Cactus Music Festival in the Minnewater Park. De Werf in the north of the city is the go-to address for jazz.

THEATRE AND DANCE

The 19th-century City Theatre (Stadsschouwburg) on Vlamingstraat is the hub of a network of cultural venues around the city, and programmes an exciting selection of Dutch-language theatre, dance, music and literature events.

Belgium's principal classical dance troupe – the Antwerp-based Royal Ballet of Flanders – brings its touring productions to the Concert Hall several times a year. Its repertoire focuses on ballet classics, but productions are far from staid: the company frequently works with contemporary artists to create ambitious staging and set design.

Contemporary dance is one of Belgium's most successful cultural exports, thanks largely to Flemish companies, many of which use live music to thrilling effect in ambitious productions. Dance has a strong local following, and the City Theatre and Concert Hall feature local and international companies with a regularity unusual in a small town.

FILM

One advantage of Dutch being spoken by little over 20 million people is that bar animation and kids' movies, films are screened in their original version, subtitled. The Lumière Cinema on Sint-Jakobsstraat and the Liberty Cinema on Kuipersstraat show everything from Hollywood mainstream to foreign arthouse movies. The Kinepolis multiplex, 5km (3 miles) south of the centre, has a larger choice. Each year Bruges hosts the excellent Cinema Nova Film Festival in March and the quirky Razor Reel Fantastic Film Festival towards the end of October.

NIGHTLIFE

Bruges has a fairly demure nightlife, with few noisy bars or rowdy crowds wandering the streets. Locals tend to prefer a quiet drink with friends at bohemian venues such as Lokkedize or De Republiek; jazz or blues in wine bars like Wijnbar Est or Vino Vino; or a late drink after a concert in the Concert Hall café. Beer fans meet at De Brugs Beertje and De Garre. Few bars in Bruges stay open really late, but those that do – including several small venues that have dance floors – are concentrated around Kraanplein, Eiermarkt and 't Zand, the last aimed more at a teeny-bopper brigade. Club nights are organised on an ad hoc basis, usually in out-of-town venues. Check bars for flyers.

HISTORY: KEY DATES

The people of Bruges have lived through invasion and occupation since records began, with fertile Flanders a favourite battleground of warring nations. Below are the key historical events that shaped the city.

EARLY PERIOD

1stC BC	Celtic farmers are established on coastal plain by what is now Bruges.
1stC AD	A Gallo-Roman settlement is founded beside the rivers Reie and Dijver, and maintains trading links with Britain and Gaul.

MIDDLE AGES

862	Baldwin I becomes first count of Flanders and occupies the Burg castle.
*c.***1040**	An English text calls Bruges an important maritime trading centre, but by the end of the century access to the sea is closed by silting.
1134	Bruges builds a canal to Damme, reopening a maritime trading route.
1250	With 40–50,000 citizens, Bruges is a large and rich city.
1297	King Philip IV of France annexes Flanders.
1302	French citizens and sympathisers are massacred in the 'Bruges Matins'. Later in the year, an army of Flemish peasants and craftsmen slaughter French knights at the Battle of the Golden Spurs at Kortrijk.

Origin of 'Bruges'
One of the first records of the name 'Bruggia' – a melding of the Old Norse *bryggja* (jetty) and Rugja, the original name of the River Reie – appears on coins of Charles the Bald in AD864. Earlier, St Eloy in Ghent wrote of the *municipium Flandrense*, an important town in the Flemish coastal plain, thought to have been Bruges.

BURGUNDIAN RULE

1384	Count Louis is succeeded by his daughter Margaret, wife of Philip the Bold, duke of Burgundy. The dazzling Burgundian century begins.
15thC	Cloth-making declines; prosperity from trade and banking continues.
1477	Duke Charles the Bold dies, succeeded by his daughter, Mary of Burgundy, wife of Habsburg Crown Prince Maximilian of Austria.
1482	After Mary's death, the Habsburg reign begins.

PROTESTANT REFORMATION

1520	Silting of the Zwin closes Bruges's sea access. Economic decline begins.
1566	Protestant 'Iconoclasts' sack churches across the Low Countries.

1580	The city signs the Treaty of Utrecht against Spain; Protestantism becomes the only permitted religion.
1584	Spain re-establishes control. Many Protestants flee to Holland.
1622	Opening of a canal to Ostend gives Bruges an outlet to the sea again.

Above from far left: Van Eyck's magnificent *Madonna and Child with Canon Joris van der Paele* (1436), now in the Groeninge Museum; signing the Treaty of Utrecht in 1715.

ENLIGHTENMENT

1715	By the Treaty of Utrecht, Belgium passes under the authority of the Austrian Holy Roman Emperor Charles VI.
1744–8	Bruges is occupied by the French.
1753	The Coupure Canal opened, allowing sea-going vessels into city centre.
1794–5	Revolutionary France invades.
1815	Napoleon defeated at Waterloo. Bruges becomes part of the Kingdom of the Netherlands under William I of Orange.

MODERN ERA

1830	Southern Netherlands revolt against Dutch rule, resulting in the formation of the Kingdom of Belgium.
1847	Hunger riots erupt in Bruges, the poorest city in Belgium.
1904	Work on the new Bruges sea harbour, Zeebrugge, is completed.
1914–18	World War I. Battles around Ypres (Ieper) are among the war's bloodiest. Germans destroy Zeebrugge harbour when they leave.
1940–4	World War II. Germans occupy Belgium.

POST-WAR, EUROPE AND FEDERALISATION

1948	Customs union between Belgium, the Netherlands and Luxembourg (Benelux).
1957	Belgium is a founder member of the European Economic Community, the forerunner of today's European Union.
1980	Establishment of Flanders and Wallonia as federal regions, and of the Flemish, French and German-speaking language communities.
2002	Bruges is European City of Culture for a year. The euro replaces the Belgian franc as unit of currency.
2011	A new Belgian government is formed after bitter negotiations between Flemish and Walloon parties lasting more than 500 days during which the country was left without a formal government – a new world record.

Belgian Monarchs
- Leopold I (1831–65)
- Leopold II (1865–1909)
- Albert I (1909–34)
- Leopold III (1934–51; abdicated)
- Baudouin (1951–93)
- Albert II (1993–present)

WALKS AND TOURS

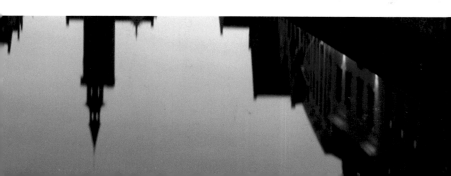

CITY HIGHLIGHTS

Prepare to pound the cobbles: this is a whistle-stop tour of the city's stellar sights, and packs the wow factor at every turn. Keep an eye out for cyclists, horse-drawn carriages and tourists looking every way except forwards.

DISTANCE 3.5km (2¼ miles)
TIME 3 hours
START Markt
END Concert Hall, 't Zand
POINTS TO NOTE
This walk is a perfect pre-breakfast wander as it is independent of opening hours (except for the Beguinage: 6.30am–6.30pm). It is also suitable for a Monday, when most museums are closed.

Bruges is a pocket-sized gem of a city and this completely outdoor circuit of its notable landmarks is ideal for a first or fleeting visit, a half-day walk that gives a sense of the layout and scale of the place. Of course, Bruges merits more than a passing glance; the subsequent 10 walks in this book explore the sights in more depth and are cross-referenced in the text below. These walks will also lead you off the beaten track to explore the hidden nooks and crannies that contain the city's real charm.

Food and Drink 🍴

① STAMINÉE DE GARRE
De Garre 1; tel: 050 34 10 29; Mon–Thur noon–midnight, Fri noon–1am, Sat 11.30am–1am, Sun 11am–midnight; €
The house brew, Tripel de Garre (10.5 percent), is wisely restricted to three glasses per person at this historic tavern.

② TOM POUCE
Burg 17; tel: 050 33 03 36; www.restaurant-tompouce.be; daily 9am–11pm; €–€€
Fish and Flemish cuisine dominate the menu at this restaurant with an unrivalled location. Order a waffle or pancake, sit on the heated terrace and watch the world go by.

③ CELTIC IRELAND
Burg 8; tel: 050 34 45 02; www.celticirelandbruges.be; daily from 10.30am; €€
A popular and friendly Irish pub/restaurant in the northeastern corner of the Burg, serving Irish and international cuisine.

MARKT

Start on the lively central square of Bruges, the **Markt** ❶ (Market Square), very much the heart of daily life in the city past and present *(see walk 4)*. The power and freedoms won by the citizens of the medieval town are embodied in the towering brick **Belfry** (Belfort), which was built between 1280–1350 and is one of the city's three great towers *(see walk 2)*. Beware here: few cafés on the square offer good value for money; if you want to admire the view, order a drink at most.

BURG

Take Breidelstraat at the southeastern corner of the Markt towards the Burg. On the way, note the narrow doorway in the wall that is ancient alley De Garre. There's a lovely beer pub here, **Staminée de Garre**, see ⑪①, to note for later if you are not ready for refreshment yet.

Smaller and more sedate than the Markt – and with only a couple of cafés, such as **Tom Pouce** and **Celtic Ireland**, see ⑪② and ⑪③ – the **Burg ❷** is the cradle of Bruges, named after the original fortified castle that founded the city *(see walk 3)*.

Several exceptional monuments and museums are located around the square, from the 13th-century **City Hall** to the famous **Basilica of the Holy Blood**.

JAN VAN EYCKPLEIN

Leave the Burg by the north, turn right on Philipstockstraat, then left on Wappenmakersstraat. Head north, crossing Sint-Jansplein to reach **Jan van Eyckplein ❸**, with historic buildings that recall Bruges's trading heyday in the 11th–13th centuries *(see walk 8)*.

Return to the Burg via Kraanrei and Kraanplein (names that recall the crane used to unload goods from incoming barges), the narrow Ieperstraat and Cordoeaniersstraat, then turn left on Philipstockstraat and right back into the Burg.

GROENEREI

Cross straight over to take the narrow **Blinde Ezelstraat ❹** (Blind Donkey Street), passing under the arch to reach the canal. The view from the bridge demonstrates why this stretch of canal is called **Groenerei** (Green Canal; *see walk 7*).

Above from far left: Bruges crest detail from the Old Recorder's House on the Burg; statue of Jan van Eyck; the Fish Market near the Groenerei canal; detail from the Belfry on the Markt.

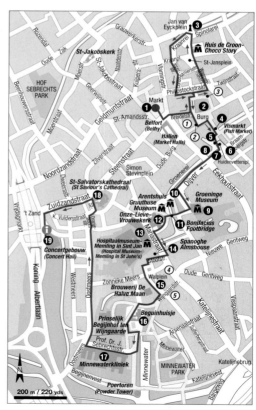

Tour of Flanders

The Markt in Bruges is the departure point each year for the prestigious Tour of Flanders cycle race, a one-day competition that has been held for over 90 years, taking place a week before the gruelling Paris–Roubaix race in spring. The race moved here from Ghent in 1998 following a bid by Bruges Mayor Patrick Moenaert, who was keen to give Bruges a reputation for something besides heritage tourism.

Ahead is the colonnaded **Fish Market** (Vismarkt); from Tuesday to Saturday, stallholders sell fish fresh from the North Sea, 10km (6 miles) away at Zeebrugge. To the right is one of several **jetties ❺** for the departure of canal boat tours. The boats all take the same route and leave many secluded stretches of water ripple-free. Walking around town, you will catch glimpses of narrow waterways overhung with trees and flanked with small gardens. There were once more waterways in the centre – many have been vaulted over – giving rise to the nickname, 'the Venice of the North'.

TANNERS' SQUARE

Turn right into the **Huidenvettersplein** (Tanners' Square; *see walk 7*), with the former **Tanners' Guildhouse ❻** (1630–1) at nos 11–12. After the tanners upped sticks, it became a freshwater fish market. Now it is lined with restaurants. Cross the square to **Rozenhoedkaai ❼** (Rosary Quay), the quayside with the most stunning vista in town.

The **mansion ❽** across the water on the bend in the canal was occupied by 16th-century Spanish magistrate Juan Pérez de Malvenda. During religious troubles from 1578–84, the relic of the Holy Blood was stored here for safekeeping. Continue walking west, keeping the bridge to your right.

DIJVER

Follow **Dijver** *(see walk 4)* to reach the main city art museum: the **Groeninge ❾**. Many of the world-class paintings in here have never left the city. From the garden leading to the museum, turn right to cross the lane named Groeninge and pass through the courtyard of the **Arentshuis ❿**, another museum. Walk diagonally to the left to cross the **Bonifacius footbridge ⓫**. To the right is the 15th-century **Palace of the Lords of Gruuthuse**, with items that evoke daily life from the 15th to 19th centuries.

MARIASTRAAT

The footpath brings you out behind the **Church of Our Lady ⓬** (Onze-Lieve-Vrouwekerk; *see walk 2*), an awe-inspiring monument from the exterior and packed with treasures inside. As you emerge onto Mariastraat, the **Hospital Museum – Memling in**

Food and Drink

④ MALESHERBES
Stoofstraat 3–5; tel: 050 33 69 24; Wed–Sun noon–1.45pm, 7–9pm; €
A small deli with dining room attached, this tucked-away eatery is good for authentic French food in an informal atmosphere. The deli is open from 10am.

⑤ CARPE DIEM
Wijngaardstraat 8; tel: 050 33 54 47; www.tearoom-carpe diem.be; Wed–Mon 7am–6.30pm; €
Wood panelling and stained glass make the perfect accompaniments to an 'olde-worlde' experience in the tearoom adjoining the Detavernier patisserie and bakery. Run by a dynamic couple, it is civilised without being over-smart.

St John's **⑬** *(see walk 5)* is across the road. Founded in the 12th century and a functioning hospital until 1976, it contains several priceless paintings by Hans Memling.

Turn left to cross the bridge. Just after, on the right, a gate in the wall leads to the secluded garden of the **Spanoghe Almshouse ⑭**, one of many historic almshouses dotted around the city, built by trade corporations or wealthy families for the poor and elderly. Visitors are welcome to enter their gardens but are asked to respect the quiet atmosphere.

WALPLEIN

Return to Mariastraat and take the next tiny lane to the right, Stoofstraat, said to be the narrowest street in Bruges, with a good lunch spot, **Malesherbes**, see ⑪④. The lane brings you to **Walplein ⑮** *(see walk 5)*, site of the sole surviving brewery in Bruges, the **Half Moon Brewery**. Cross the square to reach Wijngaardstraat, named after a vineyard once located here. Turn right – or divert to the left for an excellent tearoom, **Carpe Diem**, see ⑪⑤. On arriving at the junction with the horse drinking fountain, turn right across the bridge for one of Bruges's best-loved sights.

BEGUINAGE

An otherwordly calm pervades the courtyard of the **Beguinage ⑯** (Begijnhof; *see walk 5*), formerly home to a community of beguines – pious women who did not take the full vows of a nun. Enjoy the tranquillity of the walled enclosure: proof that even in a tiny city packed with tourists it is still possible to escape the bustle.

Pass the church and leave at the opposite side, turning left to exit the compound. You are now in the **Minnewater Park** *(see also margin)*, which is dominated by its lovely lake.

ST SAVIOUR'S CATHEDRAL

Turn right twice, into Professor Doctor Joseph Sebrechtsstraat, passing the **Minnewaterkliniek ⑰** (1908), a former city hospital and now a retirement home. Turn right at the end, on Oostmeers. This street of little terraced houses is a typical snapshot of everyday Bruges. Continue to the end, then wander on a few tiny backstreets to emerge at the rear of **St Saviour's Cathedral ⑱** (Sint-Salvatorskathedraal; *see walk 2*).

'T ZAND

Turn left on the shopping street Zuidzandstraat. This culminates at **'t Zand** *(see walk 11)*, the square that is home to the huge **Concert Hall ⑲** (Concertgebouw), with a packed cultural programme. The walk ends here, surrounded by many café options and right by the **In&Uit Tourist Office** in the ground floor of the Concert Hall.

Above from far left: 20th-century art at the Groeninge Museum; view of the bridge that leads to the Beguinage; tomb of Mary of Burgundy in the Church of Our Lady on Mariastraat.

Minnewater Toilets Worth a mention since there are so few public conveniences in Bruges, these are located on the west side of the lake. In all public toilets in Belgium, including in some cafés, you will need spare change to pay the attendant.

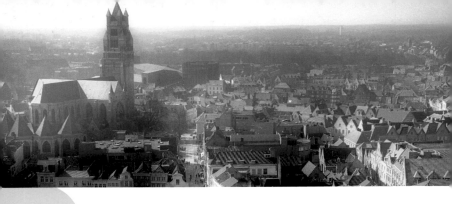

THE THREE TOWERS

Visible for miles across the flat polder landscape, the towers of the Belfry, St Saviour's Cathedral and the Church of Our Lady compete for dominance of the skyline. This walk joins the dots between the towering trio.

DISTANCE 0.75km (½ mile)
TIME 2½ hours
START Belfry
END Church of Our Lady
POINTS TO NOTE

This walk is best done in the afternoon, Tue–Fri or Sun, when all the sights are open. It can also be followed by walk 5, or preceded by it if both are done in reverse.

Like three giants parading in a Flemish folkloric parade, the octagonal tower of the Belfry, square tower of St Saviour's and pinnacle of the Church of Our Lady stalk the skyline of Bruges. Get to know their silhouettes and, wherever you are in the city, you will never be without an orientation point. This short walk introduces these three main players on the Bruges scene; their surroundings feature in later walks.

The Belfry in Film
The tower of the Belfry *(pictured right)* plays a starring role in the climactic scene of *In Bruges* (2008), and many visitors come here determined to experience the monument as seen in the film. This, unfortunately, is not possible, as it is not open to the public at night.

BELFRY

The great **Belfry ❶** (Belfort; Markt 7; tel: 050 44 81 11; www.brugge.be; daily 9.30am–5pm; charge) dominates the Markt and has long been the symbol of Bruges's civic pride, built between 1280 and 1350 after its wooden predecessor was destroyed by fire. Its upper section, an octagonal tower, was added in 1486, and leans slightly to the southeast, by a total of 1.2m (4ft) at its summit. A wooden spire that originally topped the tower was destroyed by lightning in 1493, and its replacement by fire in 1741. Today, it stands 83m (51ft) high. At its base cluster the former **Market Halls** (Hallen), a commercial centre in use

since the 13th century, now used for cultural events. In summer, bench seating is provided in the courtyard for audiences of carillon concerts.

The Climb

The only one of the three towers open to climb, the Belfry is 366 steps up, and not for the faint-hearted. On the way up is the treasury, where the magistrate's papers, town seal and charter were kept behind iron grilles (1292) which required nine keys to open them. These were held by the burgomaster (mayor) and eight trade-guild leaders, so could not be opened without the assent of all.

Further up is the 6-tonne great bell, and above that the 47-piece carillon, which peals every quarter-hour, controlled mechanically by the rotating metal drum, or, if you are lucky, by the city's own bell-ringer, who sits in a little room and plays concerts to the square. You are rewarded at the top with a 360-degree view, best in the early morning or late afternoon, of this compact city, reduced to a toy-town below.

ST SAVIOUR'S CATHEDRAL

From the Markt take Steenstraat west. As the street changes into Zuidzand-straat, you reach **St Saviour's Cathedral ❷** (Sint-Salvatorskath-edraal; tel: 050 33 68 41; www. sintsalvator.be; Mon–Fri 9am–noon

and 2–5.30pm, Sat 9am–noon and 2–3.30pm, Sun 9–10am and 2–5pm; free), the oldest parish church in Bruges. It was founded in the 9th century, but only became a cathedral in 1834 after St Donatian's, on the Burg, was destroyed. It is an unusual example of Scheldt Gothic architecture, built mainly in the 12th–15th century, but with a neo-Romanesque brick belfry, which stands 99m (60ft) tall.

Interior

Inside are tapestries, paintings and a Baroque rood-screen topped by a monumental statue of *God the Father* by Artus Quellin the Younger. Look under the late-Gothic choir stalls at

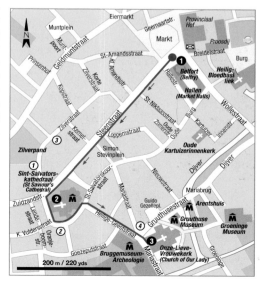

Rare Michelangelo

The Church of Our Lady contains a rare Michelangelo statue to have left Italy; it did so rather by accident. It was sold to Flemish merchant Jan Mouscron after the Italian family who commissioned it for Siena cathedral failed to pay the artist. Its stay in Bruges has not been undisturbed: although Walpole's bid to buy it for England in the 18th century failed, the French whisked it away to Paris during the French Revolution, and the Germans swiped it again in World War II.

the carved misericords (1430), and above the stalls at the coats of arms of the Knights of the Golden Fleece, who assembled here in 1478 in order to elect a new leader. Their choice, Maximilian of Austria, conferred the title from the house of Burgundy to the Habsburgs.

In the ambulatory, the first chapel clockwise contains the reliquary of Charles the Good, count of Flanders, who was killed in St Donatian's in 1127. A floor tile allegedly soaked with his blood was brought here and is said to provoke miracles when touched.

Treasury Museum

The cathedral's **Treasury Museum** (Sun–Fri 2–5pm; charge) in the southern transept contains the gory but splendid *Martyrdom of Saint Hippolytus* altarpiece, with the saint being torn limb from limb by four wild

Right: Church of Our Lady.

horses. The work is attributed to Dirk Bouts (1415–75), with one panel by Hugo van der Goes. Other paintings are by Renaissance artists Pieter Pourbus and Adriaen Ysenbrandt. As well as brass tomb-plates, reliquaries and valuable church plate, a collection of liturgical garments includes a piece of tunic that allegedly belonged to St Bridget of Ireland (*d.*525).

Dining options near the cathedral include **Cafedraal, Kardinaalshof** and **Patrick Devos 'De Zilveren Pauw'**, see ⑪①, ⑪② and ⑪③.

CHURCH OF OUR LADY

From the rear of the cathedral, take the narrow Heilige-Geeststraat southeast to the third of the city's beacons, and the tallest of the three: the **Church of Our Lady ❸** (Onze-Lieve-Vrouwekerk; Mariastraat; tel; 050 44 81 11; www.brugge.be; Mon–Sat 9.30am–5pm, Sun 1.30–5pm; free), a formidable sight with a 122m (400ft) brick spire. Built between 1290 and 1549, the church is a hotchpotch of different styles. But the church's most valuable treasures are its artworks. Chief among them is a white marble *Madonna and Child* (1506) by Michelangelo *(see margin, left)*, the first work of art to represent the Christ child as an independent person. The Madonna is a subdued, preoccupied figure, while the infant leans nonchalantly on her knee.

Church Museum

The choir, chancel and ambulatory comprise the **museum** section of the church (times as church, except closed Mon, opens 9.30am; charge), where the highlight is the side-by-side tombs of Charles the Bold and his daughter Mary of Burgundy. Whether their bodies are contained within is a matter of dispute. Charles died in battle in Nancy in 1477 and it was difficult to identify the body. Mary (who died in a riding accident aged 25, bringing to a close the 100-year reign of the house of Burgundy) may be buried in a set of frescoed tombs discovered beneath the choir in 1979 (now revealed). Either way, their sarcophagi, richly decorated in copper-gilt gold, red and blue, make for an interesting comparative study of late-Gothic and Renaissance carving: Mary's dates from 1502 and is fine and ornate; her father's from some 50 years later has far less detail. Look up from Mary's tomb to the windows in the nearby wall. This is the 15th-century oratory of the adjoining Palace of the Lords of Gruuthuse, whose wealthy residents could peer down into the church rather than attending mass with the rabble.

Notable paintings include works by Flemish Primitives Dirk Bouts and Hugo van der Goes, and a *Transfiguration* by Gerard David (*c*.1460–1523), the movement's last painter. Pieter Pourbus (1523–84) recalls the style of the earlier masters in *Last Supper* and *Adoration of the Shepherds*, while Anthony van Dyck's starkly atmospheric *Christ on the Cross* is evocative of Rubens's Antwerp school, where the master described van Dyck as 'the best of my pupils'.

If you are in need of sustenance on exiting the church, make your way to **Marieke Van Brugghe**, see ⑪④.

Above from far left: detail from the frescoed tombs in the Church of Our Lady; side-by-side tombs of Charles the Bold and his daughter, Mary of Burgundy.

Food and Drink

① CAFEDRAAL
Zilverstraat 38; tel: 050 34 08 45; www.cafedraal.be; Mon–Sat noon–3pm, 6–11pm; €€€
Just off Zuidzandstraat, an impressive collection of 15th-century buildings contains this fashionable eatery. Specialising in seafood, it is spread over two floors and has a sunny garden-terrace in the Zilverpand shopping square. Open for drinks only from 3–6pm.

② KARDINAALSHOF
Sint-Salvatorskerkhof 14; tel: 050 34 16 91; www.kardinaalshof.be; Fri–Tue, noon–2.15pm, 7–9.15pm, Thur 7–9.15pm; €€€
A smart townhouse behind the cathedral is home to this 'special occasion' favourite, where the focus is on seafood in the fixed monthly menu. Count on five or six courses for the evening meal, or three or more at lunchtime.

③ PATRICK DEVOS 'DE ZILVEREN PAUW'
Zilverstraat 41; tel: 050 33 55 66; www.patrickdevos.be; Mon–Fri noon–1.30pm, 7–9pm, Sat 7–9pm; €€€€
Star chef and wine-taster Devos runs the gastronomic show at the 'Silver Peacock'. The menu draws on fresh regional produce, complemented by top-class wines.

④ MARIEKE VAN BRUGGHE
Mariastraat 17; tel: 050 34 33 66; www.mvb.be; daily 11am–9pm, except hols; €€
Even though it is slap in the middle of tourist-ville, locals cherish this restaurant-brasserie-tearoom, which dishes up traditional Flemish fare: rabbit stew, beef cooked in beer and a great fish soup.

AROUND THE BURG

Seat of rulers and place of pilgrimage, the cobbled Burg has been the heart of civic and sacred Bruges for over a millennium. This short walk explores the historic square and its close surrounds.

DISTANCE 0.75km (½ mile)

TIME 3 hours

START Burg

END St Walburga's Church

POINTS TO NOTE

A good walk for a Monday, when many museums and other attractions elsewhere in the city are closed, but all those recommended here are open. To see the relic of the Holy Blood, time your visit to arrive at the Basilica during hours when it is presented to the public for veneration: Apr–Sept daily 11.30am–noon, 2–4pm, Oct–Mar daily 11.30am–noon, Mon, Tue, Thur 2–3pm, Fri–Sun 2–4pm. This walk could be followed by walk 6.

City Museums

The City Hall and Liberty of Bruges Palace are part of the city museum historical sites network, and may be visited using the good-value combined museum pass available from the Tourist Office.

The Burg takes its name from the town's first recorded structure: a castle on the site dating from the mid-9th century, when the Franks built a moated fort, or *burcht*, to protect against Viking marauders. This was replaced in the 11th century with a wooden residence, built for the counts of Flanders. By the Burgundian era, the city's rulers were ready for more luxurious quarters, and quit the Burg in the late 14th century for the Prinsenhof across town *(see p.69)*.

You can stand on the Burg and survey all the architectural styles that have marked the city: Romanesque, Gothic, Renaissance, Baroque and neoclassical, right up to the 21st-century steel walkway created by Toyo Ito in 2002, all within a few short paces of each other. Several of the buildings merit closer inspection, although none requires a long visit.

CITY HALL

Pride of place on the Burg goes to the three-turreted **City Hall ❶** (Stadhuis) at no. 12. The late 14th-century building is a masterpiece of Flamboyant Gothic, resplendent with detail. Once highly coloured, it is adorned with the coats of arms of local towns and villages and 34 statues (mostly copies of the originals, destroyed in the 1790s by sympathisers of Revolutionary France) representing saints, prophets and local noblemen and women.

Still mainly used for council business, only the first floor is open to the public. The **City Hall Museum** (Brugge-

museum-Stadhuis; www.brugge.be; daily 9.30am–5pm; charge) tells the story of the struggle for power in the city, between aristocrats, councillors and the population. The magnificent **Gothic Hall** has a superb polychrome, rib-vaulted ceiling and is decorated with flamboyant 19th-century biblical murals. In the adjacent **Maritime Chamber**, historic maps and engravings provide a fascinating history of the town's development. The 1562 engraving by Marcus Gerards, the earliest surviving map of the city, suggests that he must have climbed all the tall buildings in the city to get his bird's-eye view.

BASILICA OF THE HOLY BLOOD

One of the most visited sites in Bruges is tucked in the corner of the Burg at no. 10. The **Basilica of the Holy Blood** ❷ (Heilig-Bloedbasiliek; tel: 050 33 67 92; www.holyblood.com; Apr–Sept daily 9.30am–noon, 2–5pm, Oct–Mar daily 10am–noon, 2–4pm; free) comprises two chapels, one on top of the other. On the ground floor is the Romanesque **St Basil's Chapel**, built 1134–57 as the church of the long-demolished Castle of the Counts, the original residence of the counts of Flanders. The simple decor and sparse ornamentation stand in direct contrast to the **upper chapel**, which is reached from outside, via a broad spiral staircase behind a three-

arched facade, completed in 1534. Built in the 15th century, the chapel has been spoiled somewhat by the over-eager 19th-century decoration and murals, but is still impressive nonetheless. The ceiling looks like an upturned boat, while the bronze pulpit (1728) resembles a cored and stuffed tomato. The relic of the Holy Blood is preserved in a side chapel.

Above from far left: City Hall; view of the Old Recorder's House and City Hall.

Below: statue of Christ in St Basil's Chapel in the Basilica of the Holy Blood.

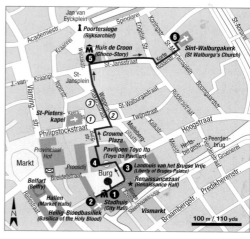

Above: the upper chapel in the Basilica of the Holy Blood.

Below: view of the Old Recorder's House from Blinde Ezelstraat.

Story of the Relic

The relic of the Holy Blood has attracted pilgrims to Bruges for over eight centuries. It consists of a phial containing what is said to be Christ's blood, washed from his body after the Crucifixion by Joseph of Arimathea. Derrick of Alsace, count of Flanders, reportedly brought the relic back from Jerusalem in 1149, having received it in recognition of his heroism during the Second Crusade. Encased in a silver and rock-crystal phial, it is dis-

played to the public each afternoon (except Wed) for veneration (for which an offering is encouraged). Many people take the opportunity to kiss it.

Basilica Museum

A side door beside the entrance to the upper chapel leads into the **Basilica Museum** (as church; charge), two rooms containing some fascinating articles, not least a reliquary (1617) made with 30kg (66lbs) of gold and silver and over 100 precious stones. A manuscript details the ceremonial garments worn by the Noble Brotherhood of the Holy Blood, which inspires participants in the annual procession today, and a 1556 painting by Pieter Pourbus showing the Brotherhood's 31 members. Other treasures include a tiny silver crown with gems that belonged to Mary of Burgundy (1457–82), which is especially dainty.

LIBERTY OF BRUGES PALACE

In the southeastern corner of the Burg is the **Liberty of Bruges Palace** ❸ (Landhuis van het Brugse Vrije), an early 18th-century building. The Liberty of Bruges was an autonomous administrative district of towns and villages outside the city, important enough to be represented from 1127 alongside Bruges, Ghent and Ypres at the Flemish Estates (a kind of early parliament). Its aldermen met in a

Palace on this site from the 14th century (much of the surviving building dates from a rebuild in 1722–7). In 1794, the Liberty was disbanded by Revolutionary France, and the palace later became the law court. Since 1988, it has been used for municipal offices.

Renaissance Hall

One early part of the building survives: the chamber where the Liberty of Bruges aldermen met, known as the **Renaissance Hall** (Renaissancezaal; www.brugge.be; 9.30am–12.30pm, 1.30–5pm; charge), which has been restored to its original condition and may be visited daily, one of 11 historical sights that form the municipal Bruges Museum (Bruggemuseum) network *(see margin, p.34)*.

It contains one of the most notable artworks in the city: a black marble fireplace and carved oak chimney-piece covering an entire wall, created in 1528–31 by Lanceloot Blondeel as a tribute to Charles V. The carving celebrates the imperial army's victory over Francis I of France at Pavia in 1525; the Treaty of Madrid, which was signed the following year, would free Belgium from French domination. The craftsmanship of the ensemble is staggering, but the brass handholds for the rural noblemen to use while drying their boots at the fire are the sort of domestic touch that everyone remembers.

ST DONATIAN'S

Head to the north of the square. The city's earliest known religious foundation – and original cathedral – stood on the tree-lined area where the modern **Toyo Ito Pavilion ❹** (Paviljoen Toyo Ito; *see margin*) is situated today. **St Donatian's**, begun around 940 and a cathedral from 1562, was destroyed in 1799–1802 by supporters of the French Revolution. In 1127, Charles the Good, count of Flanders, was murdered in the church for defending the poor against abuse by wealthy grain-hoarders.

St Donatian's was a major cultural institution in medieval times, with a great library, music school and scriptorium, where illuminated manuscripts were produced. Bookshops were clustered around the cathedral and attracted pioneers of the trade: William Caxton produced the first printed book

Toyo Ito Pavilion
Japanese architect Ito created the pavilion on the Burg to mark Bruges's year as European Capital of Culture in 2002. The open walkway occupies the site of the former central chapel in the destroyed St Donatian's Cathedral, and symbolises the link between the Bruges of yesterday and today.

Old Recorder's House

The colourful house on the Burg between the City Hall and the Liberty of Bruges Palace is the Old Recorder's House (Oude Griffie), built 1534–7. Recently redecorated in authentic bright colours typical of the period, the building is an example of the Flemish Renaissance style. The bas-relief at the top of the facade depicts the ancient Persian legend of a corrupt judge being skinned alive, a popular cautionary tale for lawmakers in medieval times (a 15th-century painting on the same theme hangs in the Groeninge Museum, *see p.44*). Today the building is occupied by law courts and is not open to the public.

in the English language in Bruges in 1473, a *Recuyell of the Histories of Troy* ordered by Margaret of York, duchess of Burgundy, before he left to introduce printing in England.

The excavated choir of the church can be explored (free; enquire at reception) in the basement of the Crowne Plaza hotel on the corner of the square.

Holy Blood Procession

The relic of the Holy Blood has been worshipped in Bruges for over seven centuries: in the past, it was said that the dried blood turned to liquid at regular intervals, a phenomenon declared to be a miracle by Pope Clement V (1264–1314). On Ascension Day every year, the relic is carried through Bruges in the famous Procession of the Holy Blood (Heilig-Bloed Processie), the most important of West Flanders's festivals, featuring 1,500 participants acting out biblical scenes, watched by 50,000 pilgrims and spectators. The bishop of Bruges himself transports the relic in an ornate gold-and-silver reliquary that is kept for the rest of the year in the chapel's museum.

REFRESHMENT OPTIONS

Now leave the Burg to the north and turn right on Philipstockstraat, where there are two good choices for eating: the successful **Het Dagelijks Brood** chain for hot drinks, snacks and light lunches at no. 21, see ①①, or, for a more substantial meal, **Baobab**, at no. 27, see ①②. Take the first left into Wappenmakersstraat, where there is yet another good lunch stop, the healthy-eating **Lotus**, see ①③.

CHOCOLATE MUSEUM

Wappenmakersstraat leads to Sint-Jansplein (St John's Square). A medieval building on the northeastern corner of the square at no. 2 Wijnzakstraat, the **Huis de Croon** is home to a privately run museum of chocolate, **Choco-Story** ❺ (tel: 050 61 22 37; www.choco-story.be; daily 10am–5pm; charge), a popular visit, though perhaps not one to be prioritised over the city's historic sights.

The museum tells the story of the cocoa bean, from its use as currency by Aztec and Maya civilisations to chocolate's status as a hot drink favoured by European royalty. Full

of information and artefacts – ancient manuscripts, porcelain, chocolate sculptures – but rather lacking in interactive features to keep children entertained, the visit concludes with demonstrations of chocolate-making and a tasting session.

ST WALBURGA'S CHURCH

Pass down the side of Choco-Story along Sint-Jansstraat, turn right at the end and then left along Korte Ridderstraat. This brings you to the front of **St Walburga's Church** ❻ (Sint-Walburgakerk; daily 10am–noon and 2–5pm; free), a Baroque oratory built by a Jesuit community in 1619–42.

Inside the Church

The cool interior is flooded with silvery light, which bounces off the riot of marble within, from the black-and-white floor tiles to the three altars and, best of all, an intricately carved Carrara marble altar-rail. A fabulously over-the-top oak pulpit (1669) competes for the wow-factor, with its double staircase and scalloped canopy upheld by trumpeting angels. Rather more discreet is a triptych with an unusual theme: *Our Lady of the Dry Tree* (1620), by Pieter Claeissens the Younger, shows the Virgin and Child perched in the branches of a tree appearing to Philip the Good, duke of Burgundy, as he

prays on the eve of battle for victory against the French.

On to St Anne's

If you want to follow this walk with another one, head down the northern side of the church, turn right at the canal on Ververdsijk and cross the first bridge to **St Anne's Church** and the start of walk 6 *(see p.52)*.

Above from far left: tempting produce at Choco-Story; St Walburga's Church.

Food and Drink

① HET DAGELIJKS BROOD
Philipstockstraat 21; tel: 050 33 60 50; www.painquotidien.com; Wed–Mon 8am–6.30pm; €
Local branch of the hit Belgian bakery and café (known as Le Pain Quotidien in French-speaking parts and abroad), which has franchised its scrubbed-pine communal table philosophy to cities around the world. Wholesome bread, dangerously addictive chocolate spreads and tarts, and generous breakfasts, but the tasty open sandwiches are not for larger appetites.

② BAOBAB
Philipstockstraat 27; tel: 050 33 14 08; www.bistrobaobab. be; Fri-Wed noon–2pm, 6.30–10.30pm, except Sat lunch and Wed dinner closed; €€
This cheerful South African bistro uses spices, coconut milk and other flavours of sunnier climes, washed down, as you would expect, with wines of the region. The meat (springbok, ostrich) and fish (tilapia, tiger prawns) are imported direct from South Africa, and there are plenty of veggie options too. Gluten or lactose intolerance can also be catered for, on request.

③ LOTUS
Wappenmakersstraat 5; tel: 050 33 10 78; www.lotus-brugge.be; Mon–Sat 11.45am–2pm; €
This long-established mainly vegetarian restaurant serves lunches only and is very popular with locals. It offers good-value, health-focused dishes, and caters for carnivores with either organic lamb moussaka or lamb stew.

MARKT TO
THE MUSEUMS

*The trading wealth of medieval Bruges found expression in a new paint-
ing technique that changed the course of Western art. Follow this walk from
the city's commercial nerve centre to its museums along the Dijver.*

DISTANCE 0.75km (½ mile), not
including distance walked in the
museums themselves

TIME A half day

START Markt

END Gruuthuse Museum

POINTS TO NOTE

The museums in this walk are
closed every Monday (apart from
Easter Monday and Whit Monday),
so it is best to do this walk on
another day of the week. This
walk can be combined with
another: follow the end point with
either walk 5, or walk 2 conducted
in reverse, starting at the Church
of Our Lady. A combined museum
pass gives cut-price entry to a
number of city-run museums,
including those covered in this walk.

Flemish Primitives

Artists working in
Flanders in the 15th
and early 16th cent-
uries were named
'Primitives' by 19th-
century art historians,
not due to any lack
of sophistication,
but because they
developed a new
technique in painting,
using oils rather than
tempera. Greatly
admired and copied
by Italian painters of
the time, their style
formed a bridge
between the art of
the medieval period
and the Renaissance.

The hub of daily life in Bruges for over
1,000 years, the Markt is the unrivalled
epicentre of activity in the city. Buses,
cyclists and horse-drawn carriages rattle
across the cobbles, dodging tourists as
they gaze skywards at the Belfry or

make a carb-crazed beeline for the fries
van *(see p.16)*. A southern detour to the
Dijver will not take you away from the
tourists, but does guarantee a succession
of aesthetic treats: from the Flemish
Primitives in the Groeninge, a medium-
sized art gallery with a global reputation,
to the turreted Gruuthuse, a 15th-
century family mansion and repository
of decorative and applied arts.

MARKT

The centre of activity in Bruges, the
Markt ❶ (Market Square) has been
the hub of commercial life in the city
since the 10th century, home to a
market since 958; one is still held every
Wednesday. In contrast with the nearby
Burg *(see p.34)*, which was the historic
centre of government and Church,
activities on the Markt have always centred around trade, as well as the odd
jousting tournament or parade.

Market Halls

The southern edge of the square is
dominated by the vast Belfry *(see p.30)*
and **Market Halls** ❷ (Hallen), built

around a central courtyard. These were the pride of the city for three centuries, a meeting place for traders from partner cities in the Hanseatic League. The existing structure was built in the 13th–15th centuries to replace its wooden predecessor, and is used today as a shopping and exhibition centre.

Provincial House

A canal now curtailed to the north, near Kraanplein, used to flow into the east side of the Markt, where a vast **Water Hall** (Waterhalle) straddled the canal, with broad quaysides for unloading goods from small barges. The neo-Gothic **Provincial House ❸** (Provinciaal Hof; closed to the public), seat of the provincial governor of West Flanders, was built on the site in 1887–92. Next door is the **central post office** (Mon–Fri 9am–6pm, Sat 9am–3pm). A new museum, **Historium** (www. historium.be), is opening on the other side of the Provincial House in Autumn 2012. It will bring Bruges' Golden Age to life though film, sounds, smells, décor and special effects.

Guildhouses and Mansions

Two notable houses stand on the west side of the Markt. The **Bouchoute House** (Huis Bouchoute; closed to the public), on the western side at no. 15, is where England's exiled King Charles II stayed in 1656–7. Built in 1480, it was restored in 1995 to the original Gothic style. Note the octagonal compass and

weathervane (1682) on the roof, which helped merchants to judge their ship's chances of entering or leaving port.

The **Craenenburg Café**, see ⑪① *(p.43)*, occupies the opposite corner of Sint-Amandstraat – a pleasant pedestrianised street with several cafés. This former residence for knights and ladies in the service of the count of Flanders offered a good view from its upper windows of tournaments held on the square.

In 1488, angry townsmen incarcerated Maximilian of Austria, widower of Mary of Burgundy, in an upper room of the house for 100 days, after he imposed new taxes on them. His advisers were tortured in rooms below, including Pieter Lanchals, his treasurer and chief mediator, who was eventually

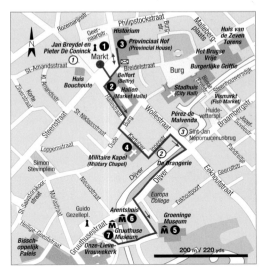

executed outside the building. The hostage-taking of the Crown Prince of the House of Habsburg (and later Holy Roman Emperor) was the final straw in a series of disputes between the people of Bruges and their rulers: Maximilian was freed after pledging to respect the townspeople's privileges, but quickly went back on his word, awarded the trading privileges to Antwerp and shifted his court to Ghent. The golden age of Burgundian Bruges was over.

MILITARY CHAPEL

Follow the west flank of the Market Halls along Hallestraat, turn right into

---

Freedom Fighters

The statue on the Markt honours two leaders of a Flemish revolt against the French, provoked by a dispute over trading rights of English wool. At dawn on 18 May 1302, butcher Jan Breydel and weaver Pieter de Coninck led an army of craftsmen from house to house, slaughtering anyone identified as French. In response, French King Philip IV raised an army of knights, who clashed with the Flemish militia two months later, on 11 July near Kortrijk. Their horses floundering in the streams and ditches that criss-crossed the field, the French noblemen fell victim to the well-organised militia; at least 1,000 knights were killed, allowing the Flemings to claim the prize that gave the conflict its name: the Battle of the Golden Spurs. Interest in the battle was renewed with the 1838 publication of the historical novel *The Lion of Flanders* by Hendrik Conscience; the statue was erected in 1887. Every year, 11 July is still marked as the official celebration of the Flemish Community.

Oude Burg then immediately left under the triumphal arch into Kartuizerinnenstraat, named after a Carthusian convent that moved into the city for protection during the religious troubles of the Reformation in 1578. A surviving part of the former abbey at the bend in the street is occupied by the city's social services department. The adjoining former church of the Carthusian nuns (1716) is now a **Military Chapel ❹** (Militaire Kapel) and war monument: its facade bears plaques commemorating people from Bruges who lost their lives in the two world wars.

DIJVER

Follow Kartuizerinnenstraat around the bend, passing the **Orangerie** hotel with its lovely terrace, see ⑪② *(and p.108)*, and join Wollestraat, which leads to the **Dijver**, a canalised offshoot of the River Reie. On the left before the bridge, at no. 35, is the 15th-century Pérez de Malvenda mansion, a shop selling Belgian specialities, with a bar, **2be**, attached, see ⑪③.

Cross the **Sint-Jan Nepomucenusbrug** (St John of Nepomuk Bridge), with a statue (1767) of the Czech martyr, who was drowned in the River Vltava (or Moldau) in Prague by King Wenceslas IV in 1393 for refusing to divulge the secrets of the confessional.

Turn right after the bridge. A small **craft and antiques market** takes place by the canal at weekends and public hol-

idays (mid-Mar–mid-Nov 10am–6pm). On the left at nos 9–11 is one site of the College of Europe, an elite, international postgraduate college for would-be eurocrats.

GROENINGE MUSEUM

A visit to the **Groeninge Museum** ❺ (Groeningemuseum; Dijver 12; tel: 050 44 87 11; www.museabrugge.be; Tue–Sun 9.30am–5pm; charge) is a highlight of any visit to Bruges. Tucked behind a garden off the Dijver, the museum traces the development of art in the Low Countries from the 15th to the 21st century, including works by the Early Netherlandish painters, or 'Flemish Primitives' *(see margin, p.40)*, who were so active in Bruges. The collection is arranged chronologically, so visitors with little time may choose to concentrate on the first few rooms.

Flemish Primitives

Jan van Eyck (1390–1441) spent much of his career in Bruges and is seen as co-founder of the movement, along with Brussels-based Rogier van der Weyden and the Master of Flemalle in Tournai. Credited with perfecting the technique of oil painting, van Eyck mixed powdered colours, egg white, water and resin to create a paint formula that allowed for a greater variety of colour and thinner application. The recipe remained a fiercely guarded secret among Netherlandish artists until the end of the 15th century.

Van Eyck's magnificent *Madonna and Child with Canon Joris van der Paele* (1436) is typical of the realism that characterised the style: characters, clothing and decoration are depicted in minute detail – the aged canon who sponsored the painting appears in particularly poor health – while at the same time the painting is dripping with symbolism, such as the colour of the robes worn by the four adult characters, which echo the heraldic colours of Bruges. The same close observation of clothing and facial detail can be seen in the *Portrait of Margareta van Eyck* (1439), the artist's wife.

Above from far left: in the Groeninge Museum; Dijver.

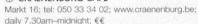

Food and Drink

① CRAENENBURG CAFÉ
Markt 16; tel: 050 33 34 02; www.craenenburg.be; daily 7.30am–midnight; €€
The best-known café in Bruges is today a traditional Flemish brasserie. A pleasant spot for breakfast, as the sunlight falls here in the morning, it serves drinks and decent food options from salads to full meals.

② MARTIN'S ORANGERIE
Kartuizerinnenstraat 10; tel: 050 34 16 49; www.martins hotels.com; daily 2.30–6.30pm
The romantic Orangerie hotel – part of the former Carthusian convent – has a charming terrace overlooking the Dijver canal to the rear. English-style afternoon tea is served daily.

③ 2BE
Wollestraat 53; tel: 050 61 12 22; www.2-be.biz; daily 11am–7pm (weather permitting)
The historic property with the most picturesque terrace in town, shaded by a weeping willow, serves drinks during shop hours, weather permitting. Given the shop's focus on Belgian specialities, this is the ideal spot to sample a local beer.

Below: details from the Groeninge Museum buildings.

Five painters developed the movement later in the 15th century, and the Groeninge houses works by four of them: Petrus Christus, Hans Memling, Gerard David and Hugo van der Goes; St Saviour's Cathedral has an important work by the fifth, Leuven-based Dirk Bouts.

Hans Memling's altarpiece painted on commission for St James's Church in Bruges, the *Moreel Triptych* (1484) is the earliest large family portrait in the Low Countries, and appears at once realistic and otherworldly. The most memorable picture for many visitors may be Gerard David's gruesome *Judgement of Cambyses* (1498), a study of a corrupt judge being skinned alive, which was hung in the Bruges city council chamber as a cautionary tale for lawmakers.

Renaissance

The fantastical world of Hieronymus Bosch, seen here in his *Last Judgement* (early 16th century), is in a class of its own, but its themes – a reflection on the fate of sinners in the afterlife – echo the economic uncertainty and malaise of the late Middle Ages.

Jan Provoost was the most significant artist of the Renaissance in Bruges; he travelled to the Holy Land and Italy, and designed the decoration for the visit of Charles V to Bruges in 1520. But his own *Last Judgement* (1525) was censored 25 years after it was painted: a detail showing damned members of the clergy was overpainted following orders from Charles V forbidding the negative depiction of churchmen and women. The offending image was only uncovered in 1965. Lancelot Blondeel and Pieter Pourbus are two other significant Bruges artists of the period whose works are also on show.

17th–18th Centuries

Paintings of the Baroque and Rococo period started to shift away from purely religious and devotional themes to more purely diverting family portraits, landscapes and still lifes, suitable for hanging in drawing rooms rather than churches. Jacob van Oost the Elder (1601–71) marked a transition point, painting altarpieces as well as portraits for the Bruges bourgeoisie. Jan Antoon Garemijn (1712–99), meanwhile, delighted in the bustle of everyday life: his Pandreitje in Bruges 1778 depicts the local street market.

19th Century

Belgium greeted independence in 1830 with a renewed search for artistic and national identity. Emile Claus (1849–1924) invented Luminism, based on Impressionism, while Antwerp painter Henry van de Velde was one of the pioneers of Art Nouveau in Belgium. Mystical Symbolism struck a chord in Bruges, a 'dead town' in the process of being rediscovered. Works by Fernand Khnopff, Leon Spilliaert and William Degouve de Nuncques show the decaying beauty of the poverty-stricken city.

20th Century

There is also a fine selection of 20th-century works, for example by Flemish Expressionists Gustave De Smet, Constant Permeke and Gustave van de Woestyne, who sought to express feelings and atmosphere through muted colours in scenes of everyday rural and industrial life. In wild contrast, they were followed by Belgian Surrealists Paul Delvaux and René Magritte, who used a realistic style to depict dreams and the unconscious mind.

A large and varied collection of post-1945 art, shown in rotation due to space restrictions, reflects the artistic styles that have flowered in the past 60 years, with works by conceptual artist Marcel Broodthaers, the Cobra movement's Pierre Alechinsky and Minimalist Amédée Cortier.

ARENTSHUIS

The **Arentshuis** ❻ (tel: 050 44 87 11; www.museabrugge.be; Tue–Sun 9.30am–5pm; charge) is a museum housed in a mansion, set in a garden neighbouring the Groeninge. Downstairs is used mainly for temporary exhibitions, often devoted to art on paper (printmaking, drawing and photography). The upper floor contains works by Frank Brangwyn (1867–1956), a Welsh artist who was an apprentice to William Morris and follower of the Arts and Crafts movement. Born in Bruges, Brangwyn

donated a large body of his work to the city in 1936. As well as decorative commissions such as murals, carpets, stained glass and furniture, Brangwyn never forgot his years as an impoverished artist, painting workers in docks and factories, and those living on the margins of society.

GRUUTHUSE

Return to the Dijver, continue west, and turn into the courtyard of the turreted Gothic **Palace of the Lords of Gruuthuse** ❼ *(see margin)*, the largest of the city's historical museums (tel: 050 44 87 11; Tue–Sun 9.30am–5pm; www.museabrugge.be; charge; the museum is undergoing major renovations until the end of 2014 so check in advance for room closures). The panelled and beamed interior offers a peek into how the wealthy lived during the Burgundian era, while the private oratory upstairs that adjoins the Church of Our Lady *(see p.32)* gives you an idea of the importance of this particular family.

The valuable and eclectic items on display – 17th-century tapestries, devotional items and sculptures, 15th-century waffle irons, articles belonging to the city guilds and even a used guillotine – evoke daily life in Bruges from the 15th to the 19th centuries, and can be best appreciated with an audioguide or by studying the information cards in each room.

Above from far left:
Arentshuis; fountain in the Groeninge Museum's garden; Gruuthuse.

Lords of Gruuthuse
The Gruuthuse Palace was built in 1465 by a powerful family that had a monopoly on the sale of *gruut*, a herb mixture used to flavour beer (the herbs are shown growing in the courtyard of nearby St John's Hospital). Lodewijk van Gruuthuse (c.1427–92) was commander of Charles the Bold's army and personal bodyguard to Mary of Burgundy. The family motto 'Plus est en Vous' (There is more in you than you think), is displayed over the door. The history of the building reflects the fortunes of the city; by 1628 it was a public pawn shop and church bank, but regained its splendour with a restoration during the Gothic revival in 1883–98.

5

MEMLING TO
THE BEGUINAGE

This walk wends its way through the beguiling south of this egg-shaped city, where time appears to have stood still for centuries. Do not leave Bruges without visiting the two highlights mentioned in the title.

DISTANCE 2.5km (1½ miles)
TIME A half day
START Archaeology Museum
END Dijver
POINTS TO NOTE
Due to the popularity of this area, try to visit early in the morning or late in the afternoon. This walk could follow on from walk 2, or before it if both are done in reverse.

Bruges Fools
To greet their new ruler Maximilian I of Austria, who married Mary of Burgundy in 1477, locals put on a big parade, dressing as revellers, jesters and fools. When, shortly after, they asked him for funds to build a *zothuis* (madhouse), he is said to have refused, with the words: 'The only people I have seen here are fools. Bruges is one big madhouse. Close the gates!'

Food and Drink 🍴
① B-IN
Zonnekemeers – Oud Sint-Jan; tel: 050 31 13 00; www.b-in.be; Tue–Sat 11am–2am, restaurant: noon–2.30pm, 6.30–10pm; €€–€€€
Club Brugge players and other local celebs like to mingle at this hip lounge bar with a lovely terrace in the pedestrianised courtyard behind St John's Hospital. It's also a restaurant, but one where style takes precedence over substance, so dress to impress. There are live DJs on Friday and Saturday.

The lush south of the city is Bruges at its most charming. Small brick houses nestle close together, their step-gables reaching tentatively up to the wide sky; secretive canals too narrow for navigation are glimpsed between houses, and nuns clad in the traditional robes of a beguine stride through carpets of daffodils on their way to prayer. Along the way are a museum with world-class paintings by Hans Memling and the only working brewery in Bruges. The narrow streets on this walk are also among the most perpetually crowded in the city, as well as the route of horse-drawn carriages, so pick your moment wisely.

ARCHAEOLOGY MUSEUM

In the former eye clinic of Old St John's Hospital, the **Archaeology Museum** ❶ (Bruggemuseum-Archeologie; Mariastraat 36a; tel: 050 44 87 11; www.brugge.be; Tue–Sun 9.30am–12.30pm, 1.30–5pm; charge) is an innovative, hands-on exploration of the development of Bruges from the Stone

Age to the present, with interactive exhibits designed around educational panels and artefacts, and with an interior styled like a real-life dig. Good fun for children.

HOSPITAL MUSEUM – MEMLING IN ST JOHN'S

Old St John's Hospital (Oud Sint-Janshospitaal) is an architectural treat, one of the best-preserved medieval hospitals in Europe, where religious orders cared for pilgrims, travellers and the sick. The large complex of buildings contains the excellent **Hospital Museum – Memling in St John's** ❷ (Hospitaalmuseum – Memling in Sint Jan; tel: **050 44 87 11**; www.brugge.be; Tue–Sun 9.30am–5pm; charge), where the highlight is a collection of paintings by German-born Hans Memling (*c.*1440–94), who lived in Bruges from 1465 until his death. Four of the six works on show were commissioned specially for the hospital chapel, where they are still displayed, by two sisters who worked here. Among them is the exquisite *Shrine of St Ursula* (*c.*1489), a wooden reliquary shaped like a Gothic church and painted with scenes from the life of the martyr. Other exhibits in the museum describe the history of medical care, illustrated with some eye-popping documents, artworks and surgical instruments.

Outside, beneath the arch to the courtyard, the former hospital **pharmacy** (same days and times but closed 11.45am–2pm) can also be visited; it contains a carved relief showing patients sleeping two to a bed. The nearby **herb garden** is planted with lady's mantle, bog myrtle and bay laurel, the herbs required to make the historic beer flavouring, *gruut*. Wander around the 19th-century hospital wards (now a conference centre) and courtyard. Overlooking the water, **B-In** is a trendy bar you might want to return to for some after-dark partying, see ⑪①.

Above from far left: canalside view of Old St John's Hospital; inside the museum.

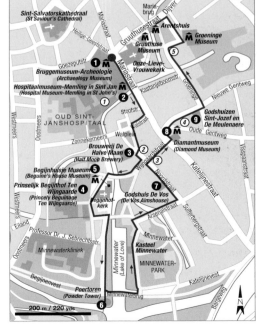

WALPLEIN

Return to Mariastraat and walk south, keeping the Church of Our Lady on your left *(see walk 2, p.32)*.

Take the second right to **Walplein**, a pretty square with cafés and touristy shops. At no. 26, the **Half Moon Brewery ③** (Brouwerij De Halve Maan; tel: 050 44 42 22; www.halve maan.be; daily 10am–6pm; charge) is the sole surviving working brewery in Bruges, and a popular tavern and brasserie, serving varied ales and food.

Records note the existence of a brewery named Die Maene (The Moon) on Walplein since 1564. This one has been run by the same family since 1856. The house brew is Brugse Zot (Bruges Fool, after the local nickname, *see margin, p.46*), created after they sold their well-known Straffe Hendrik (Strong Henry) to another producer. Guided tours (hourly, 11am–3pm weekdays Nov–Mar, Sun and summer weekdays 11am–4pm, Sat 11am–5pm) of the museum and brewery include a panoramic view from the top of the building.

Right: Half Moon Brewery detail.

BEGUINAGE

Exit Walplein at its southern end – there's an attractive eatery here, **Salade Folle**, see ①② – and turn right into Wijngaardstraat. Further down, at the green, turn right across the bridge, to enter one of the most magical spots in Bruges: the **Princely Beguinage Ten Wijngaarde** ❹ (Prinselijk Begijnhof Ten Wijngaarde; Wijngaardplein; daily 6.30am–6.30pm; free), founded in 1245 as a community for beguines: pious laywomen who, without taking lifetime vows like nuns, opted for solitude and devotion, helping the poor, teaching and preaching *(see margin, right)*.

Beguinage Enclosure

The tranquil courtyard – best seen in spring, carpeted with flowers – is surrounded by whitewashed houses, built in the 18th century to replace the original timber structures. One of 13 surviving beguinages in Belgium, recognised jointly as a Unesco World Heritage Site, the Bruges beguinage saw its last beguine leave in 1927. Since then, it has been occupied by a community of Benedictine nuns, a retreat centre and laypeople. It takes its name – Wijngaarde – from the vineyard that used to occupy this area, where grapes were grown for making vinegar. Visitors are asked to respect the quiet atmosphere within the enclosure.

Beguine's House Museum

In a small house in the corner of the courtyard, **Beguine's House Museum** ❺ (Begijnhuisje Museum; Begijnhof 30; tel: 050 33 00 11; Mon–Sat 10am–5pm, Sun 2.30–5pm; charge) recreates the living quarters of a beguine: two simple rooms with a small cloister garden and well. It is staffed by the Benedictine nuns who inhabit part of the Beguinage.

Beguinage Church

The **Beguinage Church** (Begijnhofkerk; tel: 050 33 00 11; daily 7am–12.15pm, 3–6pm; free) – full name Our Lady of Consolation of Spermalie (Onze-Lieve-Vrouw van Troost van Spermalie) – dates from 1245, but was rebuilt in 1605 following a fire, and given a Baroque makeover around 1700. The only object saved from the fire is a wooden (now gilded) statue of the Madonna (1300) on the side altar. Services held by the nuns are open to the public and include Gregorian sung offices.

Beguine History

Early beguines, many of them women of independent means, lived alone in society. They began living in walled communities in response to hostility voiced by (male) religious authorities. At a time when society had no place for women outside the family or the Church, the beguinage offered protection. An inscription over the Bruges beguinage gateway – *Sauvegarde* (safeguard) – attests to the Duchy of Burgundy's guarantee to protect the beguines and defend their independence.

Food and Drink

② SALADE FOLLE

Walplein 13–14; tel: 050 34 94 43; www.saladefolle.com; Mon–Tue, Thur–Fri 11.30am–2.30pm, 6–9pm, Sat–Sun open all day; €

In a bright, contemporary interior behind an old brick facade, this informal establishment serves a lighter menu than your average Belgian restaurant – soup, salad, quiche or pasta, including several vegetarian options – as well as dessert and ices.

Lake of Love

Victor Hugo is said to have coined the 'Lac d'Amour' title when he visited in 1837. Others say the name comes from the medieval Dutch *minne*, meaning love. Another legend has it that Minna was a Saxon maiden, whose lover returned from battle to find her dead of exposure having fled her father's house rather than marry his chosen suitor. He built a dyke and created a lake over her grave.

MINNEWATER

Cross the courtyard past the church, and exit at the southern gate, which brings you to the **Minnewater**, aka the Lake of Love *(see margin, left)*. Fringed with weeping willows, this pretty lake was once a major interior port, the Binnenwater, where up to 150 boats and barges could dock. It is fed from the perimeter and Ghent canals. The pink brick lock-house (Sashuis), built in 1519, regulates the level of water in the city canals.

Powder Tower

Walk to the end of the lake. The tower to the right of the bridge is the Powder Tower ❻ (Poertoren), a 1398 defensive tower for the former harbour, named after the gunpowder that was stocked within. Walk across the **Minnewaterbrug** (Minnewater Bridge), which gives a lovely view back over the lake.

Minnewater Park

Make your way north through the **Minnewater Park**. In summer, this lush glade is the venue for musical happenings, including, in the second week of July, the Cactus Festival, an established rock music event that draws international stars. On the left, overlooking the lake, is the Minnewater Castle (Kasteel Minnewater), a château-style former restaurant with a scenic waterside terrace (closed at the time of writing following bankruptcy). At the exit of the park, make a right turn on Arsenalstraat.

DE VOS ALMSHOUSE

Take the first left, Noordstraat. At nos 6–14, set around a beautifully tended garden, is the **De Vos Almshouse** ❼ (Godshuis De Vos), one of many such residences in Bruges, built by wealthy families from the 14th century and today maintained as homes for the elderly *(see feature, left)*. This almshouse was built in 1713 and the original eight dwellings have since been converted to six, plus a chapel.

Almshouses

The 46 almshouses (*godshuizen*) that survive in Bruges are peculiar to Flanders. They were built from the 14th century on, either by wealthy families as housing for the poor, sick or elderly, or by trade organisations for their retired members or widows. Frequently named after their benefactor, they comprised a group of tiny one-up one-down whitewashed houses, plus a chapel, shared privy and garden, a patch of which was allotted to each house. The generous donation was not made for altruistic reasons alone: rich burghers saw their charitable act as an investment that would ensure their place in heaven. Indeed, the chapels built within each complex were explicitly intended for residents to pray for the souls of their benefactors. Most of the almshouses are now owned and run by the city social services department. Visitors are free to enter the premises, but asked to respect the silence.

DIAMOND MUSEUM

Rejoin Wijngaardstraat and turn right. On the right is a simple but decent café-restaurant, **De Wijngaert**, see ⑪③.

At the top is Katelijnestraat; across the street at no. 43 is the **Diamond Museum** ❽ (Diamantmuseum; tel: 050 34 20 56; www.diamondmuseum.be; daily 10.30am–5.30pm, closed mid-Jan; charge), where you can discover the little-known local origins of diamond polishing. The technique is thought to have been invented in Bruges by 15th-century goldsmith Lodewijk van Berquem. His workshop is recreated inside, along with tools of the trade, models, paintings and rock samples; there are also daily demonstrations (12.15pm) of the technique. This private museum is run by a family in the diamond trade, whose stores are at 5 Cordoeaniersstraat and 43 Katelijnestraat.

MORE ALMSHOUSES

Walking north towards Mariastraat, if it's time for lunch or dinner there's the excellent **Indian Tandoori** restaurant nearby, see ⑪④. Then turn right into Nieuwe Gentweg to visit more adorable almshouses: the **St Joseph and De Meulenaere Almshouses** ❾ (Godshuizen Sint-Jozef en De Meulenaere) at nos 8–22. Built in 1613, they are two of the loveliest almshouses in the city, and also accessible, since their garden is usually open. Built around a shared courtyard garden with cottage-style mixed borders, there is also a tiny chapel and a water pump.

Exit the gate and cross the road. Turn directly into Groeninge, an unexpectedly bucolic lane that wends its path around the garden of the Groeninge Museum *(see p.43)* – passing a top-notch restaurant on the way, **Den Gouden Harynck**, see ⑪⑤ – and back to the Dijver, where this walk ends.

Food and Drink

③ DE WIJNGAERT
Wijngaardstraat 15; tel: 050 33 69 18; www.wijngaert.com; Thur–Tue noon–3pm, 6–10pm, café service from 11am, winter closed Wed–Thur; €
This grill restaurant, bar and tearoom along the well-worn tourist groove between the Beguinage and Onze-Lieve-Vrouwekerk is a reasonable, no-frills option for well-prepared mussels, ribs or more. The house sangria is a speciality.

④ INDIAN TANDOORI
Oude Gentweg 11; tel: 050 34 58 26; www.indiantandoori.be; Wed–Mon noon–2.30pm, 6–11pm; €–€€
The best Indian food in town, we think; although this spot is right in the heart of tourist town, it is just off the main drag and so often overlooked. Seek it out for subtly spiced, authentic dishes from the Subcontinent, made with the freshest ingredients and served with understated grace.

⑤ DEN GOUDEN HARYNCK
Groeninge 25; tel: 050 33 76 37; www.goudenharynck.be; Tue–Fri noon–2pm, 7–9.30pm, Sat 7–10.30pm, closed last week of Dec, one week at Easter, three weeks from mid-July–early Aug; €€€€
Taking its name from the 17th-century former fishmonger's shop that it occupies, this luxurious restaurant is the showcase for chef Philippe Serruys. A master of French gastronomy, Serruys draws on Bruges's trading past to mingle local and exotic flavours to fantastic effect.

SINT-ANNA

The quiet district of Sint-Anna is famed for its small-scale and offbeat attractions: a crusader's mausoleum, ancient crossbowmen's club, lace centre, windmills and museums of folklore and poetry. At a relaxed pace, you could spend the best part of a day ambling around here.

DISTANCE 2.5km (1½ miles)

TIME 3 hours

START St Anne's Church

END Café Vlissinghe

POINTS TO NOTE

This walk could follow on from the end of walk 3, by crossing the Sint-Annabrug to reach the start. It is a good walk for children, as the Folklore Museum has much to keep them entertained, and – for all but tiny ones – the windmill is fun. Tue–Sat is the ideal time to do this walk, and definitely avoid Sun, when the Jerusalem Church, a highlight, is closed.

Jerusalem Church Tower
Outside, the tower is capped with a Jerusalem cross and the wheel and palm leaf of St Catherine, to commemorate the journey of Anselm and his son to Jerusalem and Mount Sinai in 1470.

In a quiet neighbourhood removed from the centre, the Sint-Anna district has few shops or cafés, and is characterised by rows of simple terraced houses and a faintly bucolic air. Ideal for a stroll, it offers an insight into the history of everyday life in Bruges. Peek inside a former almshouse, discover the gruelling lot of a lace-maker and peep over high walls into the crossbowmen's club. Then relax on a grassy canal bank with a beer.

SINT-ANNA

Start on Sint-Annaplein at **St Anne's Church ❶** (Sint-Annakerk; Apr–Sept Mon–Sat 10am–noon and 2–5pm, Sun 2–5pm; free), a 1624 Baroque edifice, with ornate carving inside. The counter on the left as you enter used to be where the poor of the parish would mark registers each time they attended mass, so they could receive tokens for food and clothing on feast days. Leave the square at the eastern end, and then turn right into Jeruzalemstraat.

Jerusalem Church

The striking **Jerusalem Church ❷** (Jeruzalemkerk; Peperstraat; tel: 050 33 00 72; www.kantcentrum.com; Mon–Fri 10am–noon, 2–6pm, Sat until 5pm; charge, includes entry to Lace Centre) was built in 1428–65 by a family of Genoan merchants based in Bruges. Pieter Adornes returned from a pilgrimage to the Holy Land to build this copy of the Church of the Holy Sepulchre and his son Anselm completed it. A mixture of Byzantine and Gothic styles, it has been spared

destruction thanks to its private chapel status and is remarkably well preserved, boasting 16th-century stained glass.

Anselm was murdered in Scotland in 1483 while on a diplomatic mission and was buried in Linlithgow, but his heart was brought back to Bruges to be laid to rest beside his wife, Margaretha. Their black marble sarcophagus dominates the interior; later generations of the family are buried beneath the church and recalled in coats of arms on the walls. An altar carved with skulls and bones and a copy of Christ's memorial tomb in the crypt complete the deathly atmosphere.

Lace Centre

On the same entrance ticket as the Jerusalem Church, the **Lace Centre** (Kantcentrum; details and times as Jerusalem Church) is a non-profit foundation that organises lace-making courses and holds demonstrations of the craft of bobbin lace every afternoon. Examples of lace-work are displayed off the courtyard in six tiny almshouses that the Adornes family built for the poor in the 15th century. Around the corner, at no. 11 Balstraat is a shop, **'t Apostelientje** (tel: 050 33 78 60; Mon–Sat 9.30am-12.15pm, 1.15-5pm, Sun 10am–1pm), selling local handmade lace articles as well as craft supplies.

Museum of Folklore

Walk north up Balstraat. Near the end, at no. 43, is the **Museum of Folklore ❸** (Bruggemuseum – Volkskunde; tel: 050 44 87 11; www.brugge.be; Tue–Sun 9.30am–5pm; charge), in a row of 17th-century whitewashed cottages that were once the almshouse of the **Shoemakers'** Guild. Each room

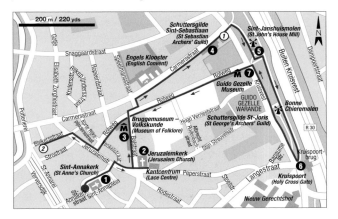

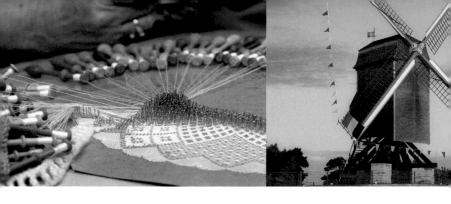

Ring Canal Park
The park adjoining
the canal that
encircles the city
along the line of the
former ramparts was
created in 1876 on
the initiative of Count
Amédée Visart de
Bocarmé. The long-
serving mayor of
Bruges was a great
believer in green
spaces, and said:
'I've planted many
trees in my life.
I believe now
that planting and
re-planting forests is
the most productive
cultural activity that
one can do.'

reconstructs a 19th-century interior: a primary-school class, clogmaker's and milliner's workshops, a pharmacist and a confectioner (with sweet-making demonstrations on Thursday afternoons) among others. In summer, visitors can play with traditional toys and games in the garden; and the visit ends, charmingly, in an old ale house, **The Black Cat** (De Zwarte Kat).

English Convent

At the top of Balstraat, cross Rolweg and continue straight up Speelmans-straat, turning right on Carmersstraat. On the left at no. 85 is the **English Convent** (Engels Klooster; tel: 050 33 24 24; www.the-english-convent.be; daily 2–3.30pm, 4.15–5.30pm), established in the wake of England's Dissolution of the Monasteries under

King Henry VIII. The convent and its church were a hub for the city's former English colony, which in the 1860s numbered 1,200. It is now a guesthouse for groups and individuals on retreat.

St Sebastian Archers' Guild

Further up Carmersstraat at no. 174 is the skinny hexagonal tower of the **St Sebastian Archers' Guild ④** (Schut-tersgilde Sint-Sebastiaan; tel: 050 33 16 26; www.sebastiaansgilde.be; May–Sept Tue–Thur 10am–noon, Sat 2–5pm, Oct–Apr Tue–Thur and Sat 2–5pm; charge). This ancient longbow club dates from the time of the Crusades; past members include England's King Charles II, who paid for the ban-queting hall while in exile in Bruges from Oliver Cromwell. Charles formed a royal regiment of guards here, which accompanied him to London when the monarchy was restored in 1660. All British monarchs since have been hon-orary members of the guild, whose collection contains arms, furnishings, gold and silver plate, and other artworks.

At the top of Carmersstraat are a couple of pleasant cafés, including **De Verloren Hoek**, see ⑪①.

ST JOHN'S HOUSE MILL

The green space ahead is dominated by the **St John's House Mill ⑤** (Sint-Janshuismolen; Kruisvest; tel: 050 44 81 11; www.brugge.be; May–Aug Tue–Sun 9.30am–12.30pm, 1.30–5pm, Sept

---

Food and Drink 🍴

① DE VERLOREN HOEK

Carmersstraat 178; tel: 050 33 06 98; Thur–Mon 10.30am–9pm (kitchen noon–2pm, 6–9pm), Tue 10.30am–2pm; €
This friendly neighbourhood café has a green outlook, facing the ring canal park and the St John's House Mill. Its laid-back terrace and simple bar food – salads, omelettes, steaks and snacks – make it a popular spot in fine weather.

② CAFÉ VLISSINGHE

Blekersstraat 2; tel: 050 34 37 37; www.cafevlissinghe.be; Wed–Sat 11am–midnight, Sun 11am–7pm; €
Founded in 1515, this is the oldest café in Bruges, with wood-panelled walls, long oak tables and a good-sized garden. The beer list is not impressive and the bar food is simple, but this is an institution: come here to relive the Bruges of yore. It tends to stay open as long as the punters keep drinking on Fri and Sat.

Sat–Sun 9.30am–12.30pm, 1.30–5pm; charge), one of four timber-stilt windmills that dot the canalside park *(see margin, p.54)* along the northeastern city perimeter, left here as a reminder of the 29 that once dotted the ramparts, mainly milling grain. During the summer months, this particular mill, which earned its living from 1770–1914, is cranked back into action and open to the public. Access is via a vertiginous staircase.

HOLY CROSS GATE

Walk south through the park past the next mill, Bonne Chieremolen (not open to the public), to the **Kruispoort** ❻ (Holy Cross Gate), one of the entries to the city from the second town wall of 1297. This structure dates from the early 15th century, but has been much rebuilt. Seen from outside, the gate has two fortified towers, joined by a battlement through which stones or molten lead could be dropped on invaders. In contrast, from within the walls residents saw an elegant portal, with octagonal turrets and dripstone moulding.

GUIDO GEZELLE MUSEUM

Retrace your steps north. On the left is another old archery club set in a garden, visible by its tall target-mast. Unlike at St Sebastian's, the chaps of **St George's Archers' Guild** (Schuttersgilde Sint-Joris; Stijn Streuvelsstraat

59; tel: 050 44 87 11; open by prior arrangement only) are crossbowmen.

Continue up Kruisvest and turn left on Rolweg. At no. 64, the **Guido Gezelle Museum** ❼ (tel: 050 44 87 11; www.brugge.be/musea; Tue–Sun 9.30am–12.30pm, 1.30–5pm; charge) is the childhood home of the poet-priest (1830–99). Gezelle fought to establish Flemish as a literary language distinct from Netherlandish Dutch. His life and work are recalled in the house, and the large walled garden is charming.

Café Vlissinghe

Follow Rolweg to the end, turn right onto Jeruzalemstraat, and second left on Blekersstraat. The oldest café in Bruges, **Vlissinghe**, see ⑪②, can be found down this narrow street, a fitting place to end this walk.

Lace-Making in Bruges

By the mid-1800s, Bruges was the poorest city in Belgium, dependent on home-based textile manufacture and unable to compete with industrialised cities. In the 1840s, the lace-making industry provided steady employment – and starvation wages – for 10,000 women and girls (nearly a quarter of the population). They worked 12 hours a day yet still needed to resort to prostitution to pay for food. Today, most lace sold is machine-made and imported, although some is still hand-made locally. The most popular kind of lace made in Bruges is bobbin lace, created using a technique where threads of silk, linen or cotton on as many as 700 bobbins are crossed and braided around a framework of pins. For a handmade lace veil or tablecloth, count on paying upwards of €400.

FISH MARKET
TO ASTRID PARK

This tour takes in a succession of scenic quaysides, along canals punctuated with lichen-covered bridges. It then follows a waterway through a laid-back former industrial quarter to end in a park much loved by locals.

> **DISTANCE** 2km (1¼ miles)
> **TIME** 1½ hours
> **START** Fish Market
> **END** Astrid Park
> **POINTS TO NOTE**
> This walk has no attractions with paying entry, so any day is suitable. It is ideal for a dry day, as it is almost entirely outdoors. It is also good for children, as it ends in a park with a playground.

It is a sign of how compact Bruges is that on this relatively short walk you can wander from the most photographed view in the city to an ignored stretch of canal where the houseboats and grassy banks make it feel like a country village, a world away from coach parties and tour-boat megaphones. In fact, it is not far at all, and that is the beauty of Bruges: step away from the hubbub and there's a relaxed small town going about its business with an enviable quality of life.

Food and Drink

① DE VISSCHERIE
Vismarkt 8; tel: 050 33 02 12; www.visscherie.be;
Wed–Mon noon–2pm, 7–10pm; €€€€
The flavours of the sea are cooked to perfection in this top-notch fish restaurant, where the maître d' will attend to your every whim. Ideal for special occasions or formal dining with all the frills. A few meat dishes are also available.

② WIJNBAR EST
Braambergstraat 7; tel: 050 33 38 39; www.wijnbarest.be;
Wed–Mon 4pm–midnight; €€
In a city short on nightlife, this wine bar is popular with locals, with its daily menu of wines served by the glass, 90 varieties on the menu and live music on Sunday evenings. Light and main meals are also served.

FISH MARKET

The neoclassical, colonnaded **Fish Market ❶** (Vismarkt), built 1820–1, is one of few notable structures dating from the period of Dutch rule *(see box, p.59)*. From Tuesday to Saturday mornings, fishmongers lay out the morning's catch fresh from nearby coastal ports Zeebrugge and Ostend. Right alongside, restaurant **De Visscherie**, see ⑪①, is the go-to address for fish and seafood specialities. Craft stalls occupy a number of the stands at other times.

ROSARY QUAY

Leave the Fish Market by the south, turning right on Braambergstraat. This takes you past two eating and drinking options for now or later, **Wijnbar Est**, see ⑪②, and **De Gastro**, see ⑪③ *(p.59)*, to one of the most picturesque spots in Bruges: the view over the canal basin from **Rozenhoedkaai ②** (Rosary Quay), an idyllic spot by day or night. Winston Churchill is one of many artists, amateur and professional, to have painted the scene from this spot, picking out the warm patina of medieval brickwork reflected in the canal, capped by the view to the Belfry

beyond. The maudlin protagonist in Georges Rodenbach's novel *Bruges-la-Morte* occupied a house on this quayside, which in turn inspired the 1906 poem 'Quai du Rosaire' by Rainer Maria Rilke.

TANNERS' SQUARE

Retrace your steps a little and turn left into **Huidenvettersplein ③** (Tanners' Square). Between Easter and October, the small square is packed with restaurant tables and street painters. The former Tanners' Guildhouse (1630–1) on the west side of the square is now an upmarket restaurant, 't Huidevet-

Above from far left: Rosary Quay; coat of arms on the former Fishmonger's Corporation House, Tanner's Square; view of St Saviour's Cathedral from the Groenerei; dried fish at the market.

Boat Tours
The small armada of open-topped motorboats that tour the central canal network offer a unique view of the city. The boats, many of which come with an English-speaking guide, operate daily from Mar–Nov 10am–6pm, and at weekends and holidays in winter. Boats depart from Rozenhoedkaai, Steenhouwersdijk, Dijver, Nieuwstraat and Mariastraat. Warm clothing is advised, and you will need to duck when passing under low bridges.

tershuis. Cross the square and exit at the northeastern corner. On the left, the house alongside the jetty is the former **Fishmongers' Corporation House**; note the fishy coat of arms above the door.

GROENEREI

This is one achingly pretty stretch of canal. Keep the canal to your left, passing the Fish Market on the right. The view across the water shows the rear of the Town Hall and the surviving 16th-century facade of the Liberty of Bruges Palace, which from the Burg side is hidden by an 18th-century addition. Continue along Steenhouwersdijk, which turns into tree-lined **Groenerei**. Pass **Meebrug** and **Peerdenbrug**, two stone bridges that create lovely reflections beneath their arches. Stand on Peerdenbrug to admire the view back to the tower of St Saviour's Cathedral. On the right, at nos 8–12, the **Pelican Almshouse ❹** (Godshuis De Pelikaan) can be identified by the relief of a pelican (a symbol of Christ) feeding its young. Built in 1634, it was an almshouse and hospital for the poor.

ALONG THE COUPURE

Follow the narrow canalside path as it bends right, passing the lovely Het Hemelhuis sauna *(see margin)* at no. 16. The tourist boats peel off left to the north, while we head south towards a more tranquil quarter of the city. Cross Predikherenstraat and continue straight over alongside the water. This wider portion of canal, the **Coupure**, reflects its industrial heritage. It was dug in 1752 to allow river traffic from Ghent a shorter route via Sint-Annarei to the Langerei, bypassing the winding waterways through the centre. It retained an industrial character until the start of World War II. The southern end is a popular mooring spot for houseboats and cabin cruisers, and for fishermen trying their luck from the quay.

Bistro Option

Turn left to cross the **Coupurebrug** (Coupure Bridge) and then right to follow the canal's eastern bank south. If it's time for a meal, make the most of a good spot on the corner by the bridge, **Bistro de Schaar**, see ⑪④.

Conzett Bridge

On the grassy square a little further south is a small statue of a girl, *Marieke*, inspired by the character in Jacques Brel's song 'Ai Marieke'. At the end, turn right to cross back across the water via the modern **Conzettbrug ❺** (Conzett Bridge), a cycle- and footbridge designed by Swiss engineer Jürg Conzett to mark Bruges's year as European Capital of Culture in 2002. Scrolls of rusting metal span the walkway of weather-washed timber, forming a handy link in the park.

Heavenly Sauna

The Hemelhuis (Heaven House; tel: 050 67 96 93; www. hemelhuis.be; Sept–May Thur and Fri 1.30–10.30pm; Sat 12.30–6pm; June–Aug Thur and Fri 5.30– 10.30pm; Sat 12.30– 6pm; charge; private hire also possible) is a beautiful sauna and hammam, where Moorish lamps and mosaics add warmth to the cool post-industrial design. Mixed nudity is the rule, as is typical for saunas in Belgium, but there is a women-only slot on Tuesdays.

GHENT GATE

Continue along the footpath leading southwest from Conzettbrug to the **Ghent Gate** ❻ (Gentpoort; Thur–Sun 9.30am–12.30pm, 1.30-5pm; charge), one of four surviving medieval city gates that served a dual role as fortification as well as to monitor imports and exports in and out. An exhibition inside tells the history of the city's gates.

ASTRID PARK

Turn back towards the city centre up Gentpoortstraat, a local shopping street, to the southern tip of **Astrid Park** ❼ (Astridpark). Named after Queen Astrid (1905–35), the Swedish-born consort of King Leopold III who died tragically young in a motor accident, it is one of the largest parks in the city, with a pond, kids' playground and a colourful bandstand. The park is still known among locals as the 'Botanieken Hof', recalling its origins as a botanical garden when it was created in 1850 on the site of a former Franciscan friary. The **St. Magdalene's Church** (Heilige Magdalenakerk) (1851–3) sits on the southern corner of the park.

Park Café

A pleasant café, **L'Estaminet**, faces the northern edge of the park at the end of this walk, see ⑪⑤.

Dutch Rule

After Napoleon's defeat at Waterloo in 1815, the Congress of Vienna united the Northern and Southern Netherlands under the Protestant rule of William I of Orange in an effort to create a strong buffer against France. This union, after 200 years of separation, was especially unpopular in Catholic Bruges, among all but a small Protestant minority. Within 15 years, the Southerners organised a rebellion in Brussels, which Dutch forces barely attempted to suppress. When it declared independence in 1830, the Southern Netherlands became Belgium, a self-governing region for the first time in its history.

Food and Drink

③ DE GASTRO
Braambergstraat 6; tel: 050 34 15 24; www.degastro.be; Thur–Tue 11am–11pm; €–€€
This stylish address has concocted a menu to please all comers, from snacks to Belgian classics and fusion-inspired dishes, while pancakes and waffles are served all afternoon. Prices are lower than the decor and smart presentation suggest.

④ BISTRO DE SCHAAR
Hooistraat 2; tel: 050 33 59 79; Fri–Wed noon–2.30pm, 6–10pm; €€
This rustic bistro is a good alternative to the tourist-focused city-centre restaurants. A popular neighbourhood eatery, it has an open grill-fire and specialises in grilled fish and meat. Locals reserve tables, so it is wise to do the same.

⑤ L'ESTAMINET
Park 5; tel: 050 33 09 16; Mon–Wed, Fri–Sun 11.30am–late; Thur 4pm–late; €
Open since 1900, this family-friendly café gets packed on a Sunday afternoon, after the obligatory park stroll. A laid-back establishment, it serves good-value and tasty spaghetti Bolognese and other simple bar meals, plays the blues and sometimes hosts live music.

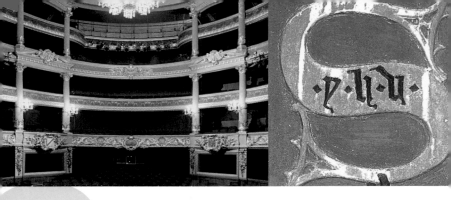

MERCHANTS' QUARTER

The hub of international trade in the 14th century has numerous landmarks that evoke the city's commercial heyday. This walk is not only a journey back in time; it is a reminder that markets that rise must also fall.

DISTANCE 1.5km (1 mile)
TIME 2½ hours
START/END City Theatre
POINTS TO NOTE
This walk starts and ends very near the Markt, just up Vlamingstraat to the north. It has few indoor sights on its route, so take an umbrella if the weather looks inclement.

By the 14th century, Bruges's cloth-making industry was in decline. Commerce became its fortune: as a member of the Hanseatic League, it drew merchants from Castile, the Rhine, Genoa and London, along with Italian bankers, who controlled the flow of finance. This walk visits the district where they lived, met and exchanged goods: sheepskin, lead and tin from England and Scotland, wine, spices and luxury products from Italy, and citrus fruits, leather and sugar from Spain. Much of the city's artistic and built heritage dates from this period: trade brought revenue through taxes, and local residents grew wealthy providing services to the cosmopolitan visitors.

Papageno Statue
The bronze statue in front of the theatre is of Papageno, the bird-fancier from Mozart's *Magic Flute*; a copper-engraved score from the same opera is set in the pavement across the street.

CITY THEATRE

Our starting point is a more recent building, the **City Theatre ❶** (Stadsschouwburg), built in 1867 in neo-Renaissance style by Brussels architect Gustave Saintenoy. Until the Concert Hall was built in 2002, this was the prime arts venue in town; today, it is the hub of an arts network, as likely to show classical theatre as world music or contemporary dance.

Across the road from the theatre is the tempting **Patisserie Servaas van Mullem**, see ⑪①.

MERCHANTS' HOUSES

The square at the junction of Academiestraat and Vlamingstraat was a meeting place for merchants and traders from the 13th–16th centuries. The **Genoan Lodge ❷** (Genuese loge) at no. 33 dates from 1399; the city's coat of arms is still visible above a small side door. The bell-shaped gable was added in 1720 when the building passed to a federation of serge traders from Hondschoote near Dunkirk – hence its name, **White Serge Hall** (De Witte Saaihalle).

Fries Museum

The building is now occupied by the **Fries Museum** (Friet Museum; tel: 050 34 01 50; www.frietmuseum.be; daily 10am–5pm except two weeks mid-Jan; charge), devoted to the history of potatoes and chips. An important part of this history entails restoring to Belgium ownership of a food known widely as 'French fries', allegedly the result of confusion on the part of American soldiers after World War I.

Ter Beurze House

Medieval merchants who could not get bed space in their own consulate were housed by locals such as the Van der Beurze family, whose 1453 **Ter Beurze House** (Huis Ter Beurze) stands at no. 35. (The facade was restored to its original style in 1947.) Such families became middlemen, introducing buyer and seller, and acting as lenders, guarantors and exchange agents until the deal was cut under their roof. This house became synonymous with the practice, giving its name to places throughout Continental Europe where merchants met to fix prices for the exchange of goods: *beurs* (in Dutch) and its equivalents in other languages: *bourse*, *börse* and *bursa*. Now home to a local radio station, this was the world's first stock exchange.

Venetian and Florentine Houses

Neither the Venetian consulate at no. 37 nor the Florentine lodge at Academiestraat 1 has survived, but their memory lives on in an **engraving** from canto 15 of Dante's *Inferno* on the side wall of the latter address (now a restaurant, **De Florentijnen**, see ①②) describing Bruges's perpetual battle with the sea: 'Even as the Flemings, 'twixt Cadsand and Bruges,/ Fearing the flood that tow'rds them hurls itself,/ Their bulwarks build to put the sea to flight.'

Above from far left: City Theatre's opulent interior; detail from Ter Beurze House; Papageno statue; City Theatre exterior.

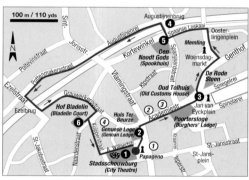

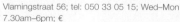

Food and Drink

① PATISSERIE SERVAAS VAN MULLEM
Vlamingstraat 56; tel: 050 33 05 15; Wed–Mon 7.30am–6pm; €
Well-dressed professionals and academic types take their morning coffee over a paper at this upmarket patisserie with a tempting spread of cakes and tarts. There is a small terrace alongside the shop, facing the theatre.

② DE FLORENTIJNEN
Academiestraat 1; tel: 050 67 75 33; www.deflorentijnen.be; Tue–Sat noon–2pm, 7–10pm; €€€
This sleek and stylish modern eatery takes its inspiration from the earlier use of the building by Florentine merchants. It has a lively buzz and dishes up classy Italian-French food, with painstaking attention to presentation.

JAN VAN EYCKPLEIN

Turn right into Academiestraat, passing **Brasserie Forestière**, see ⑪③, a good dining option, to **Jan van Eyckplein** ❸, named after the 15th-century painter who made his name in Bruges. Stand by his statue, which has its back to the canal, for a view over these sights.

On the western side of the square is the tower of the 15th-century **Burghers' Lodge** (Poortersloge), a meeting place for bankers and merchants. From elite club *(see margin, right)*, the building became a fine arts academy until 1890; today, it houses the city archives.

Old Customs House

Across Academiestraat from the Burgher's Lodge is the pointed gable of the **Old Customs House** (Oud Tolhuis),

where ships had to pay taxes on goods brought into Bruges from the outer ports of Damme and Sluis. Behind its facade is a 13th-century merchant's house, with spacious rooms on lower floors for storing goods, and living quarters upstairs. The tiny house next door was the 15th-century HQ for porters *(pijnders)*. Their back-breaking trade is evoked in stone carvings at the base of a pillar. Next door was the public weighing house. The combined buildings are now the seat of the provincial library, which holds 600 religious manuscripts and early printed books.

Spiegelrei and Spinolarei

Turn around to face the canal. Bruges has many former harbours and this one – along **Spiegelrei** and **Spinolarei** – was one of the busiest: the canal once continued to the Markt. Porters would have unloaded Castilian oranges and lemons, oriental spices, Mediterranean velvet, and Baltic fur and amber. This was the diplomatic centre of Hanseatic Bruges, with foreign consulates situated along Spiegelrei. Many of the houses retain vast vaulted storage cellars.

De Rode Steen House

At no. 8 on the square, on the corner of Spiegelrei, is **De Rode Steen**, a house that partly dates from the 13th century. This was the first building in Bruges awarded renovation funding, in 1877, marking the start of investment to restore the city's heritage. On the right

---

Food and Drink 🍴

③ BRASSERIE FORESTIÈRE
Academiestraat 15; tel: 050 34 20 02; www.brasserie
forestiere.be; Mon, Tue, Thur 11.30am–6pm, Fri–Sat
11.30am–3pm, 6–10pm; €
Reasonably priced, laid-back restaurant in an elegant
town house with marble fireplaces and bare wooden tables,
recently expanded into the property next door. Light meals
– pasta, quiche, salads, including vegetarian options – are
served by friendly, young staff.

④ VINO VINO
Grauwwerkersstraat 15; tel: 050 34 51 15; Tue–Sun
6pm–late; €
Sangria, Spanish tapas, blues on the sound system and
a friendly owner have earned this backstreet wine bar a
faithful following. Good for a romantic tête-à-tête, it is also
one of the few nightlife options in town.

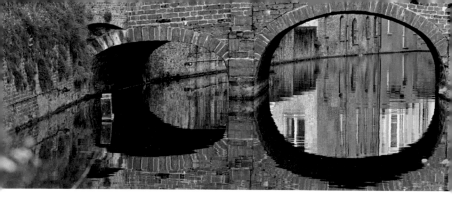

Above from far left:
Spiegelrei with
Jan Van Eyckplein
to the left; Augustin-
ians' Bridge.

of the steps to the door is a plaque hon-
ouring Georges Rodenbach *(see p.57)*,
whose grandfather lived nearby. Keep
this house on your right and head northeast up Genthof. Note the rare surviving
16th-century timber facade at no. 7.

SPANISH QUAY

Walking northeast, cross Woensdag-
markt, named after a former Wednesday
vegetable market. A **statue of Hans
Memling** (1871) by Hendrik Pickery
now has pride of place. Then cross
Oosterlingenplein (Easterners' Square)
and turn left alongside the canal into the
Spaanse Loskaai (Spanish Quay),
where Spanish ships used to dock,
unloading bundles of Castilian wool.

Augustinians' Bridge
Triple-arched **Augustijnenbrug** ❹
(Augustinians' Bridge) was the first
stone bridge in Bruges, built in 1294
by monks from a friary then situated
by the canal. Legend has it there was
once a tunnel under the canal by which
monks would reach a convent on the
other bank, for illicit trysts with nuns.

Phantom House
The House of Lamentations (Den
Noodt Gods Huis) ❺ on the west
corner of Spanjaardstraat beside the
bridge was built in 1616 by Spanish
merchant Francisco de Peralta. Since
the 19th century, it has been known as
the **Phantom House** (Spookhuis),

inspired by stories of a monk who killed
the object of his devotion in a fit of pas-
sion. Their two spirits allegedly haunt
the building, which has changed hands
repeatedly, and been abandoned on
more than one occasion.

Cross Augustinians' Bridge for a walk
along some attractive canalside streets.
Turn left on Augustijnenrei, cross Sint-
Jorisstraat and continue straight on
Pottenmakersstraat. Turn left at the end,
crossing back over Ezelbrug to the south
side of the canal, and turn left into
Grauwwerkersstraat, which follows the
canal and then bends to the right.
Remember this street if you fancy some
tapas at **Vino Vino**, see ⑪④.

BLADELIN COURT

Around the bend, turn right into Naar-
denstraat. The **Bladelin Court** ❻ (Hof
Bladelin) at no. 19 was built around
1440 by Pieter Bladelin, treasurer to
Duke Philip the Good and his Order of
the Golden Fleece. The Medici Bank of
Florence took over the property in 1466,
and gave it an Italianate makeover. This
can be seen in the **inner courtyard
garden**, the only part of the building
open to the public (Mon–Fri 9am–
noon, 2–5pm; free). Stone medallions
on the courtyard facade depict Lorenzo
de' Medici and his wife, Clarice Orsini.
It is now a home for senior citizens.

Retrace your steps and turn right into
Kuipperstraat. This leads to the rear of
the theatre, where this walk began.

White Bear Club
Among visitors to
the Burghers' Lodge
were members of the
illustrious White Bear
(Witte Beer) Club,
whose emblem can
be seen in a niche
on the corner of the
building. According
to legend, the white
bear was the first
inhabitant of Bruges
and caused terror
in the region until
Baldwin Iron Arm,
first count of
Flanders, nailed it
to a tree in the 9th
century. It figures,
with the lion, on the
city's coat of arms.

LANGEREI AND ST GILES

Follow Langerei, a canal that used to be the city's trading lifeline, passing old bridges and an abbey to an ancient hospital museum and church, and returning via a sleepy quarter once favoured by stars of the early Flemish art scene.

DISTANCE 2.5km (1½ miles)
TIME 2½ hours
START Carmersbrug
END Café Terrastje
POINTS TO NOTE

Mainly outdoor and quite long, this walk is best done on a fine day. It could be combined with an excursion to Damme, by boat, cycle or on foot (walk 12), or followed by walk 6 in Sint-Anna conducted in reverse, or linked with the shorter walk 8 in the Merchants' Quarter.

Below: Duinenbrug, a wooden drawbridge across the Potterierei.

Furs, amber, flax and honey were among the imports to medieval Bruges from its partners in the Hanseatic League, an alliance of trading cities and guilds that operated from the 13th to the 17th century. As silting progressively restricted direct access to the sea, ships would dock in the outer port of Damme, 7km (4½ miles) away, and then Sluis, when the route to Damme became impractical. From there, small barges would convey goods into the city along Langerei.

POTTERIEREI

Set off from the **Carmersbrug ❶** (Carmelite Bridge). Note, on its south-eastern side, the carved stone monk who measures the depth of the water with his staff. Turn left and follow Potterierei north.

Imported goods including coal, wheat and wood were unloaded along the Langerei canal right up until World War II. The tranquil **Potterierei**, which snakes north up its eastern quayside, is still lined with historic properties; it looks its best in the afternoon sun, when dappled light filters through the plane trees that line the quay.

Episcopal Seminary

Pass the next bridge, Snaggaardbrug, and, further up, the wooden drawbridge, **Duinenbrug**. The latter takes its name from the former Cistercian **Abbey of the Dunes** ❷ (Ter Duinen Abdij) at no. 72. The abbey moved to Bruges in 1627 from its previous location in Koksijde; it was threatened by encroaching seas. Following the French Revolution, when the abbey became public property, the buildings were used successively as a military hospital, military depot and a school. In 1833, it was returned to the Church and has become the **Episcopal Seminary** (Groot-Seminarie), a college for Catholic priests.

Our Lady of the Pottery

Further up at no. 79 is the 14th-century **Our Lady of the Pottery** ❸ (Onze-Lieve-Vrouw-ter-Potterie; Tue–Sun 9.30am–12.30pm, 1.30–5pm; free). Once the chapel of the Potters' Guild, the church was part of a hospice founded 1276 by Augustinian nuns. Much of the complex is still a retirement home, although today's residents occupy modern buildings.

The unusual church has a double nave; the older, to the north, dates from 1359. The embroidered hangings (*c*.1565) in the side altars contain gold and silver thread, while the south nave holds possibly the oldest Netherlandish miracle statue, *Our Lady of Mons-en-Pévèle*, crafted in wood in the early

14th century and named after the 1305 battle from which it takes its name. The 16th-century tapestries flanking the left side of this nave depict miracles associated with the Virgin Mary.

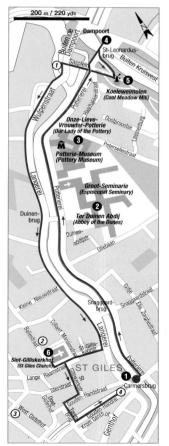

Above from far left:
Potterierei; Our Lady
of the Pottery.

Canal Rules

Private boats are banned on the canals *(reien)*, which look mirror-smooth on quiet stretches such as Gouden-Handrei and in low season, when the tour boats cease plying the waters. Properties along the waterside do not suffer the same degradation as in areas of tidal sea water (such as Venice), but can request that the water level is lowered periodically (usually in winter) to allow maintenance below the waterline.

Above from left:
St Giles Church;
Cool Meadow Mill;
Gouden-Handrei.

The **Pottery Museum** (tel: 050 44 87 11; Tue–Sun 9.30am–12.30pm, 1.30–5pm; www.brugge.be; charge), in the church's former wards and cloisters, displays medical artefacts that recall the former hospice, plus furniture, Delftware, tapestries and a glittering array of church plate and rare manuscripts.

Food and Drink

① BISTRO DU PHARE

Sasplein 2; tel: 050 34 35 90; bar Wed–Mon 11.30am–late; food 12.30–3pm, 6pm–midnight; www.duphare.be; €€
This music bar-brasserie has a friendly atmosphere, varied menu (Creole, Thai, steaks) and live blues and jazz bands. Busiest at night, but a pleasant spot for lunch or drinks. A large south-facing terrace beside the canal is a draw.

② 'T OUD HANDBOGENHOF

Baliestraat 6; tel: 050 33 19 45; Tue–Sat 6–10pm, Sun noon–1.30pm, 6–10pm; €€
Push the heavy door to this ancient hostelry and enter a Brueghelian scene: a beamed dining room with gigantic fireplace, flagstone floor and hearty Belgian cuisine, from steak, fish or mussels to snacks like omelettes and toasted sandwiches. The garden to the rear is shady in fine weather.

③ TOM'S DINER

West Gistelhof 23; tel: 050 33 33 82; Wed–Mon 6pm–1am; www.tomsdiner.be; €€
Although slightly off our route, this place is highly popular with locals, with exposed brick walls, candlelit setting and a late kitchen, serving a successful blend of international influences.

④ TERRASTJE

Genthof 45; tel: 050 33 09 19; Sun–Tue 11am–11.30pm, Wed 11am–7pm, Fri–Sat 11am–midnight; €€
This tiny café with a larger terrace, run by an English-Dutch couple, is prized for its varied menu: soup, snails, *waterzooï*, omelette and salads, plus nibbles (ham and cheese platters) and desserts (ices and pancakes).

DAMPOORT

Continue to the end of Potterierei and **Dampoort ④**, the former gate on the road to Damme. Pleasure cruisers and industrial barges wait here for the road-bridge to be raised over the ring canal. After the waterway to the Zwin inlet silted up, a new canal to Ostend was opened in 1622. Many large vessels today take the more recent **Boudewijnkanaal** (1896–1905) to Zeebrugge.

Cool Meadow Mill

The **Cool Meadow Mill ⑤** (Koeleweimolen; June–Sep Tue–Sun 9.30am–12.30pm, 1.30–5pm; www.brugge.be; charge) stands beside the canal on Kruisvest, south of the bridge. Built in 1765, it is part of the city museum network and an operating grain mill open to the public in summer.

LANGEREI

Return to Dampoort and cross to the western bank of the Langerei canal via Sasplein, south of the busy road junction. At no. 2 is a handy refreshment stop, the **Bistro du Phare**, see ⑪①. Wander back south along Langerei, admiring the bourgeois mansions that line the canal. There is little to detain you here, although if you fancy a break, step off the street at no. 76, where an alley leads to a small garden with picnic tables behind the houses.

ST GILES

After passing the Snaggaardbrug on the left, take the next right, Sint-Gilliskoorstraat. This is St Giles district, for centuries home to workers and artists, including Jan van Eyck, Hans Memling and Gerard David. Later, along with the St George's (Sint-Joris) district to the west, it was something of an English colony. Art historian James Weale (1832–1917), who is credited with discovering the works of Memling and other Flemish Primitives, lived at the junction of Sint-Jorisstraat and Clarastraat. Still a largely residential district, it retains an air of quiet detachment from the rest of the city.

St Giles Church

Entered via its western door on Baliestraat, **St Giles Church** ⑥ (Sint-Gilliskerkhof; Mon–Sat 10am–noon, 2–5pm, Sun 2–5pm; free) was founded in 1241. Major alterations in the 15th century left it with three aisles in place of its earlier cruciform; only the chunky stone pillars inside date from the original construction. The painter Hans Memling was buried here in 1494 in the long-gone churchyard, and is remembered by a plaque located beside the entrance.

Among the treasures inside are a superb organ, a polyptych (1564) by Pieter Pourbus and a cycle of paintings from 1774 by Bruges artist Jan Garemijn, depicting the history of the Trinitarian Brothers and their retrieval of white slaves from Algeria.

Food Options

If you are thinking about food at this stage, **'t Oud Handbogenhof** offers authentic Flemish cuisine and atmosphere, see ⑪②. Alternatively, seek out **Tom's Diner**, see ⑪③.

GOUDEN-HANDREI

From the southern side of the church take Sint-Gilliskerkstraat. At the end, turn right along Gouden-Handstraat. An English seminary used to be situated on this street. Turn left onto Torenbrug. The property on the left beside the bridge (now part of the College of Europe) was where painter Jan van Eyck lived and worked, entertaining wealthy patrons in his studio.

Over the bridge, turn left to follow the quayside of **Gouden-Handrei** back to the start of the walk. This stretch of canal is enchantingly still, reflecting the gardens and summer houses of the historic properties on the opposite bank. The light is at its best in late afternoon.

Café Stop

At the end of the street, turn right towards the Carmersbrug, where this walk began. It ends at the next junction, with Genthof, where there is a pleasant café, **Terrastje**, see ⑪④.

Bricked-Up

Although the terraced houses in St Giles are very small, many have had windows bricked up. This practice dates back to 1800, when a window tax was levied.

PRINCES' COURT
AND DONKEY GATE

The dukes of Burgundy called this district home at the height of their rule in the 15th century. This walk takes in the site of their former palace, a quiet park and a church adorned with treasures donated by noblemen and merchants.

DISTANCE 3km (2 miles), or short version 1.75km (1 mile)
TIME 1–2 hours
START/END Eiermarkt
POINTS TO NOTE
The shorter version of this walk excludes a few non-essential sights, including the Donkey Gate. Visitors should also note that St James's Church, one of the highlights of this walk, is not open from October to March.

The period of Burgundian rule in Bruges from 1384–1482 was a time of both prosperity and tension, marked by the Hundred Years War between England and France and by power struggles between the aristocracy and the trade guilds. While its rulers were at war with England, business depended on imports of English wool for cloth production. International traders in the city tired of the incessant quarrelling and, by 1457, the Hanseatic League had shifted its headquarters to Antwerp, depriving the

city of precious income from banking and inn-keeping. In place of cloth, the city started producing luxury items such as illuminated manuscripts, miniatures, panel paintings and cut diamonds. Bruges remained fabulously rich, thanks in part to the Burgundian court's support of the arts, but the source of its wealth – trade – had started to ebb away.

MUNTPLEIN

From **Eiermarkt** (Egg Market), with its 1761 pump adorned with the lion of Flanders and the Bruges bear from the city's coat of arms, take Geldmuntstraat to Geerwijnstraat, first right, which leads to **Muntplein ❶**. Named after the count's former coin mint *(munt)*, this small square contains an equestrian statue – *Flandria Nostra* – depicting Mary of Burgundy, who died aged 25 in 1482 after a riding accident. Crushed when her horse reared while out hunting, Mary's death signalled an end to Burgundian rule in Bruges: her husband, Maximilian I of Austria, a Habsburg, was an unpopular ruler who decamped with his court to Antwerp.

PRINCES' COURT

From Muntplein, rejoin Geldmunt-straat (*geld* means money) via the arched former gate, turn right, then right again at the next street, into Prinsenhof. The **Prinsenhof 2** (Princes' Court; *see p.111*), now an upscale hotel, is a neo-Gothic copy (1888) of the palace of the dukes of Burgundy, built in 1396 on this site. In its original form, the palace was seven times the size of what you can see, and stretched from Noordzandstraat to Moerstraat, surrounded by walls and battlements.

History of the Princes' Court
Philip the Good married Isabella of Portugal here in 1430 and founded the Order of the Golden Fleece to mark the event. The wedding banquet was held in a hall decorated with tapestries made of gold thread. Every dish was delivered on a gold platter, while jousting entertained the guests outside. In 1468, on the occasion of his marriage to Margaret of York, Duke Charles the Bold put on a vast pageant, which is re-enacted to this day (*see feature, p.71*). Sorrow began to shroud the palace after the violent death of Charles in 1477. After his daughter Mary died just five years later, the palace – and Bruges – fell from favour. The Habsburgs put it up for sale in 1631, and it passed into the hands of a Franciscan order, before being largely destroyed under French rule at the end of the 18th century.

MINSTRELS' CHAPEL

Leave Prinsenhof at the northwest, turning right on Ontvangersstraat, then left along Moerstraat. At the end, turn right across the canal into Been-houwersstraat. On the left side north of the bridge is the former **Minstrels' Guild Chapel** (Speelmanskapel), built in 1421 and now owned by a private foundation, used for cultural events.

Above from far left: neo-Gothic Princes' Court; Donkey Gate.

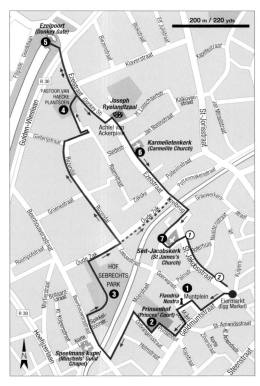

Hof Sebrechts Park

The tranquil park was originally the vegetable garden of the Sisters of St Elisabeth Convent, which stood nearby from the 15th–18th centuries. The park takes its name from Joseph Sebrechts, a surgeon at Sint-Janshospitaal (now the Memling Museum), who bought the property in 1928 and hired a landscape architect to create the garden. Now a public park, it has a sandpit and children's play area and, in summer, a sculpture exhibition.

HOF SEBRECHTS PARK

A gateway in the wall on the right of Beenhouwersstraat leads into **Hof Sebrechts Park** ❸ (Mon–Fri 9am–dusk, Sat–Sun and hols 10am–dusk; free), a tranquil oasis behind houses (*see margin*).

Exit the park on Oude Zak. The following section of the walk contains no unmissable sights, but offers a pleasant detour via another small garden to a city gate. To shorten the walk, continue to the end of Oude Zak, then turn right to cross the canal and right again to St James's Church (*see below*).

PASTOR VAN HAECKE GARDEN

For the longer walk, turn left from Oude Zak onto Rozendal, a residential street in a quarter of Bruges that few tourists explore. At the end, turn right, then immediately left on Raamstraat. This appears to be a dead end, but a gate in the wall leads into a shady **garden** ❹ named after Pastor Van Haecke (1829–1912). This curate of the Basilica of the Holy Blood and sacristan of Saint James's Church caused controversy and was accused of Satanism. The garden is densely planted with trees and shrubs around a small pond. Exit through the gate on the eastern side to emerge onto Ezelstraat (Donkey Street).

EZELSTRAAT

Turn left and walk to the **Ezelpoort** ❺ (Donkey Gate), which dates from 1369–70 but has been frequently rebuilt since. Return towards the city and walk south on Ezelstraat. Set back from the street on the tiny Achiel van Ackerplein is the Joseph Ryelandtzaal, where a ghostly sculpture of a conductor's hands protrudes from the wall. Now a concert hall named after local composer Joseph Ryelandt (1870–1965), this was once the convent church of the Carmelites.

Carmelite Church

Further down the street, at no. 28, is the 15th-century **Carmelite Church** ❻ (Karmelietenkerk; www.priorij.be; Mon–Fri 8am–11.30am, 3–5.30pm; free), attached to the priory of Discalced (or 'Barefoot') Carmelite Fathers that has occupied the former **Hof van Uitkerke** here since 1633. They were expelled by the French in 1795 but returned in the 19th century, and the church is one of the few places in Bruges still used by a religious order. Every Sun at 10am there is a sung Gregorian mass; the church is also used for concerts regularly. Its peaceful Baroque interior (1688–91) is lined with confessionals.

ST JAMES'S CHURCH

Continue over **Ezelbrug** (Donkey Bridge) and follow the road round to the right. Just after the bend, but

entered via its west door, is **St James's Church** ❼ (Sint-Jacobskerk; Apr–Sept Mon–Sat 10am–noon, 2–5pm, Sun 2–5pm; free), once the richest parish church in Bruges. Built from 1220, the church grew in the 15th century thanks to generous donations from its wealthy parishioners: the Burgundian court and other merchants and courtiers. Little of its medieval character is visible today, as the interior is dominated by Baroque features added in the late 17th and early 18th centuries. However, each of the 18 altars was sponsored by a trade guild or corporation; note Lancelot Blondeel's 1523 altarpiece for the Surgeons' and Barbers' Corporation.

Other artists who created paintings for the church include Hans Memling, Hugo van der Goes and Rogier van der Weyden. One remains: the triptych of *The Legend of St Lucy* (1480), painted by a Memling contemporary known as the Master of the Legend of St Lucy, who has been identified as the author of dozens of other works. This altarpiece tells the story of a wealthy Sicilian virgin who, in gratitude for the recovery of her sick mother after a pilgrimage to St Agatha's tomb, gave all her worldly goods to the poor. This displeased the man to whom she was betrothed and he had her condemned to death.

There are also two triptychs by Pieter Pourbus, and the mausoleum of Ferry de Gros (1544), treasurer of the Order of the Golden Fleece, which is one of the finest examples of Flemish Renaissance sculpture.

Return to Sint-Jakobsstraat and head south back to Eiermarkt. On the way, drop in at one of two refreshment options, **Wereldcafé de Republiek** or **In Den Wittenkop**, see ❶① and ❶②.

Above from far left: Golden Tree Pageant; exterior detail from the Carmelite Chuch.

Golden Tree Pageant

The Golden Tree Pageant (Praalstoet van de Gouden Boom) recalls the festivities held during Charles the Bold's marriage to Margaret of York in 1468. After a wedding ceremony conducted in Damme, the duke paraded his fair bride into Bruges to enjoy days of feasting and tournaments. Named after the prize awarded to the winner of the tournament on the occasion, the pageant evokes the lives of the counts of Flanders and dukes of Burgundy, followed by a re-enactment of the wedding procession. Held every five years since 1958, usually in late August, the next pageant is in 2017.

Food and Drink

① WERELDCAFÉ DE REPUBLIEK
Sint-Jakobsstraat 36; tel: 050 34 02 29; daily 11am–late; www.derepubliek.be; €
This bohemian café of the Cultuurhuis de Republiek (which includes the Lumière art-house cinema) has a large interior courtyard. Besides drinks from coffee to cocktails, fresh food is prepared up to 11pm, after which a limited choice is available.

② IN DEN WITTENKOP
Sint-Jakobsstraat 14; tel: 050 33 20 59; Tue–Fri noon–2pm, 6–9.30pm, Sat 6–9.30pm; www.indenwittenkop.be; €€
Lined with retro advertising panels, this bistro is run by a stylish, friendly couple. Although the cuisine is officially French, the menu includes Belgian standards such as *waterzooï* – made with langoustines rather than white fish or chicken. There is a lush terrace to the rear.

AROUND 'T ZAND

Set out from the striking Concert Hall for this short circular walk around a neighbourhood dotted with whitewashed almshouses, a chapel for the blind and a lush stretch of the ring canal.

DISTANCE 1.5km (1 mile)
TIME 1 hour
START/END 't Zand
POINTS TO NOTE

This itinerary covers an area between the station and 't Zand, where the tourist office is located. It could easily be appended to either walk 2 or 10, joining at their nearest points. It is best done in the afternoon as Our Lady of the Blind is open 2–5pm only.

Food and Drink

① 'T PUTJE

't Zand 31; tel: 050 33 28 47; www.hotelputje.be; daily 8.30am–11pm; €€
Facing the Concert Hall, the crisp tablecloths and smart wicker chairs set this hotel brasserie apart from the nearby run-of-the-mill pavement cafés. Reliable French and Belgian classics are served from breakfast until late.

② CONCERTGEBOUWCAFÉ

't Zand 34; tel: 050 47 69 99; www.concertgebouw.be; Wed–Sat and before and after performances, 11am–late; €
This cultural pitstop on the ground floor of the concert hall is ideal for lunch. The food is straightforward, well presented and filling, and the sound system samples highlights from the month's concert programme.

This segment of Bruges is separated from the city centre, sandwiched between the ring road and the perimeter canal. The hinge that keeps it connected is the 't Zand (Sand Square), site of the original railway station. Today it is dominated by the modern Concert Hall, where the acoustics and musical programme are as remarkable as the architecture. To its west is a typical residential neighbourhood, ideal for a stroll to explore a small chapel, park and almshouses.

'T ZAND

A square used for jousts, executions and tournaments from its earliest days, **'t Zand** is a focal point on the edge of the city, enlivened by funfairs, a Saturday market, the tourist office and cafés frequented more by locals than tourists, such as **'t Putje**, see ⑪①. The ring road has been buried beneath ground in recent years, allowing the square to be reclaimed as a pleasant public space.

Sculpture Fountain

In the centre is a bronze **sculpture fountain ❶** (1985–86) by artists

Stefaan Depuydt and Livia Canestraro. The figures depict four themes: cycling; the polder landscapes of Flanders, especially the village of Damme; fishermen, to signify the city's dependence on the sea; and four bathing women symbolising the cloth towns of Bruges, Ghent, Antwerp and Kortrijk.

Concert Hall

A striking example of contemporary architecture in a city that thrives on the past, the **Concert Hall ②** (Concertgebouw; tel: 050 47 69 99; www.concertgebouw.be; open during performances) was designed by Paul Robberecht and Hilde Daem to mark the city's year as European Capital of Culture in 2002. The exterior is clad in 68,000 terracotta tiles, a nod to the red-brick architecture of medieval Bruges. The interior is minimalistic, with bare concrete walls, and a particularly original Chamber Music Hall, where the audience sits in single rows arranged vertically in a square spiral around the stage. Known especially for its early music repertoire, the concert hall also programmes contemporary dance and new music.

On the top floor, the **Sound Factory** (Tue–Sun 9.30am–5pm; charge) is a museum space offering visitors the chance to experiment with different sound installations, including the old bells from the Belfry Tower, whilst admiring one of the best views of the city.

The **In&Uit Tourist Office** (tel: 050 44 46 46; www.brugge.be; daily 10am–6pm) is situated in a ground-floor wing of the concert hall, as is an airy café, the **Concertgebouwcafé**, see ⑪②.

OUR LADY OF THE BLIND

Follow the shopping street of Smedenstraat west. The fourth street on the right, Kreupelenstraat, leads to a quaint chapel, **Our Lady of the Blind ③** (Onze-Lieve-Vrouw van Blindekens; Kreupelenstraat; daily 2–5pm; free). Founded to honour a promise made at the battle of Mons-en-Pévèle in 1304 against the French (which

Above from far left: cafés on 't Zand; salami at the Saturday market; sculpture fountain on the square.

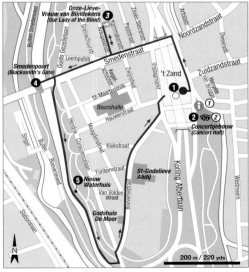

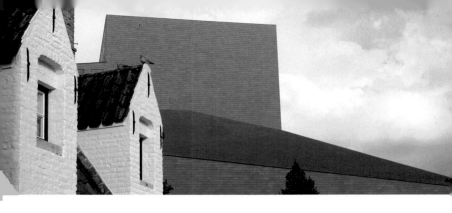

Above from left:
the terracotta tiles of
the Concert Hall;
cycling along
the Damme Canal.

resulted in a treaty granting Flemish independence), the church dates from the 17th century. Its most precious artefact is a gilded 14th-century statue of the *Madonna and Child*, above a side altar. The chapel is the departure point for the annual Feast of the Assumption procession, every 15 August, to Our Lady of the Pottery on Potterierei *(see p.65)*.

Take the alley alongside the chapel towards Kammakersstraat and peep into the neat courtyard gardens of the Van Pamel, Marius Voet and Laurentia Soutieu almshouses *(godshuizen)*, built for the blind.

BLACKSMITH'S GATE

Below:
the old Belfry bells at
the Sound Factory.

Back on Smedenstraat, walk west to reach the **Smedenpoort** ❹ (Black-

smith's Gate), built in 1367–8 and with 17th-century modifications. The bronze skull recalls the Ghent citizen who betrayed Bruges in 1688 by trying to open the gate to French invaders, led by Louis XIV.

NIEUW WATERHUIS

Turn south on the city side of the bridge into the park that follows the line of the former ramparts, parallel to Hendrik Consciencelaan. The small brick building in the park is the **New Water House** ❺ (Nieuw Waterhuis), a pumping station used from the 14th–18th centuries, when a horse-actioned pump distributed drinking water across town.

BOEVERIESTRAAT

At the end of the park, head north up Boeveriestraat, lined with former almshouses, some dating from the 14th century. The **De Moor Almshouse** at nos 52–76 was founded in 1480 for aged stonemasons, carpenters and coopers; while **Van Volden Almshouse** at no. 50 occupies the site of a medieval hospital for foundlings and mentally ill children.

Near the top on the right at nos 5–19 are the tiny 15th-century Van Campen, Van Peenen and Gloribus (17th century) almshouses, which look too small to be inhabited by anyone but hobbits.

DAMME

The pretty village of Damme, 7km (4 miles) northeast of Bruges, was a major trading outpost in the Middle Ages. Hire a bike or walk up the tree-lined Damme Canal (Damse Vaart) canal for an easy half-day excursion.

Damme rose to prominence when a major coastal flood and tidal wave in 1134 enlarged the Zwin inlet and permitted sea-going vessels to sail to this tiny settlement. A canal was dug to Bruges, and Damme became the city's principal outer port, where ships would transfer their cargoes onto smaller boats to enter the city.

As the village grew, it enjoyed great affluence and patronage. When French King Philippe-Auguste captured and razed the town in 1213, his entire fleet of 1,700 ships could be contained in the former harbour. The town was quickly recaptured by the Flemish and a frenzied building period began, including the first fortifications. Damme remained a strategic stronghold for centuries after the sea channel silted up in 1280, when the port relocated upstream to Sluis. A second city wall was built in the early 15th century.

In recent years, the village has made the most of its literary connections, re-inventing itself as a book village. Its picturesque canalside setting, popular with strollers and cyclists, makes it a favourite destination for a Sunday lunch jaunt; thus, in addition to bookshops, Damme is well stocked with restaurants.

DISTANCE 1.25km (¾ mile)

TIME A half day

START Town Hall

END Old ramparts

POINTS TO NOTE

To get to Damme, 7km (4 miles) northeast of Bruges, either cycle or walk up the Damme Canal from Dampoort or take no. 43 bus from Bruges ('t Zand, Station or Markt; Apr–Sept and school holidays daily, Oct–Mar Wed only; 20 min). The paddle steamer *Lamme Goedzak* (Apr–mid-Oct; www.bootdamme brugge.be; 35 min) departs just north of Dampoort at Norweegse Kaai 31 every two hours. If walking, you could also arrange to take a taxi one way.

TOWN HALL

Begin on the main **Marktplein** (Market Square), where the diminutive **Town Hall ❶** (Stadhuis; not open to the public) was rebuilt in 1464 and has remained largely intact since. The facade niches contain figures such as Joan, Countess of Flanders (1199–1244), who gave permission for the Stadhuis to be

Book Village
As well as several bookshops selling new and second-hand volumes, a Book Market takes place on Marktplein in front of the Town Hall every second Sunday of the month. Damme's earliest known literary connection is celebrated on the same square – the statue here is of Jacob van Maerlant (1230–96), the 'father of Dutch poetry', who lived in Damme from around 1270 and wrote his most important works here.

Napoleon Effect
The town's size shrunk by a half under Napoleon Bonaparte, who in 1811 used Spanish prisoners-of-war to dig a canal from Bruges to the Scheldt, destroying numerous patrician mansions and the old Corn Market.

built, and Charles the Bold and Margaret of York, who married here in 1468. The belltower contains 25 bells, a sundial and a clock from 1459. On a fine day, the south-facing terrace of **Pallieter** next door is tempting, see ⑪①.

TIJL UILENSPIEGEL MUSEUM

On the southeastern side of the square, the 15th-century house **De Grote Sterre** was home to Spanish governors during the 17th century; today, it contains the **Tourist Office** and **Visitor Centre** (Jacob van Maerlantstraat 3; tel: 050 28 86 10; www.toerismedamme.be; mid-Apr–mid-Oct Mon–Fri 9am–noon and 2–6pm, Sat–Sun from 10am,

mid-Oct–mid-Apr until 5pm and Sat–Sun pm only). Also here, the **Tijl Uilenspiegel Museum** (as Tourist Office; charge) is devoted to the 14th-century German folk-tale character Uilenspiegel, who has been adopted by the town as a mascot. In an 1867 novel by Charles De Coster, Uilenspiegel is born in Damme and leads the resistance against the Spanish occupiers.

HERRING MARKET

Walk east on Jacob van Maerlantstraat, then turn right on Corneliestraat. Opposite the junction, **De Lieve**, see ⑪②, is one of the town's best restaurants. Corneliestraat leads to the former **Herring Market ②** (Haringmarkt), where a reputed 28 million herring were processed annually in the 15th century – hard to imagine in this tranquil square, bordered by whitewashed houses.

ST JOHN'S HOSPITAL

Retrace your steps a little, taking the first left, Pottenbakkersstraat, to reach Kerkstraat, the main road through the village. **St John's Hospital Museum ③** (Museum Sint-Janshospitaal; tel: 050 46 10 80; www.ocmw-damme.be; Easter hol–end Sept Mon 2–6pm, Tue–Thur and Sat–Sun 11am–noon, 2–6pm; charge) stands at no. 33. Endowed in 1249 by Margaret of Constantinople as a hospice, and financed by the town's income from a tax on wine, the main

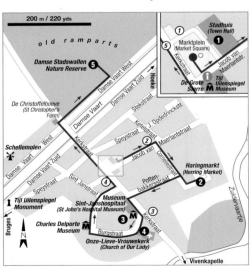

building is Gothic, but other parts are of a later date. The museum, in the chapel and infirmary, contains furniture, paintings, silverware, documents and other items chronicling daily life in Damme.

Tante Marie, see 🍴③, at no. 38, is good for a snack or light meal.

CHURCH OF OUR LADY

Continue south along Kerkstraat to a path on the right leading between pollarded trees to the part-ruined **Church of Our Lady** ❹ (Onze-Lieve-Vrouwekerk; tel: 050 28 86 10; May–Sept 10.30am–noon and 2.30–5.30pm), a squat Gothic edifice from around 1340. Climb the flat-topped **tower** (charge) for a view over the village, fortifications and surrounding polder. Continue through the churchyard to exit on Burgstraat, which loops back to rejoin Kerkstraat. Walk back northwest past the Marktplein. On the way are **De Damse Poort** and **De Drie Zilveren Kannen**, see 🍴④ and 🍴⑤.

OLD RAMPARTS

Damme remained a military fortress centuries after the decline of Bruges. It was on the frontline of the war between the Spanish and Dutch in the 16th–17th centuries, and the Spanish fortifications, in the shape of a seven-point star, are still discernible. Most of the moats were later filled with earth during building of the new Damme Canal

under Napoleon Bonaparte *(see margin, opposite)*. See what remains by crossing the bridge and turning right. The small **Nature Reserve** ❺ on the left has a path that leads among the **old ramparts**.

Food and Drink

① PALLIETER
Kerkstraat 12; tel: 050 35 46 75; www.pallieterdamme.be; Tue–Thur and Sat–Sun summer 10am–10pm, winter 11am–7pm; €
Perfect for people-watching, this café-restaurant's terrace often gets packed. Inside is just as nice, with warm red walls and fresh flowers. Specialities include steak and fish dishes.

② DE LIEVE
Jacob Van Maerlantstraat 10; tel: 050 35 66 30; www.delieve. com; Wed–Sun for lunch and dinner, Mon lunch only; €€€
In this highly regarded gourmet restaurant, owner-chef Frank Verstraete draws on the best of French and Belgian influences, with a forte for fresh fish and a clever way with herbs.

③ TANTE MARIE
Kerkstraat 38; tel: 050 35 45 03; www.tante-marie.be; Sat–Thur 10am–6pm; €
This country-style tearoom and lunch restaurant serves mouth-watering pastries and light meals, including salads and local specialities like prawn-stuffed tomato. The weekday fixed-price lunch with champagne is a treat.

④ DE DAMSE POORT
Kerkstraat 29; tel: 050 35 32 75; www.damsepoort.be; Thur–Tue 10am–10pm; €€
A smart old farmhouse with an elegant dining room and large back garden. Serves Flemish staples with a seafood bent – eels, oysters, prawns and sole – and teas between meals.

⑤ DE DRIE ZILVEREN KANNEN
Marktplein 9; tel: 050 35 56 77; Wed-Sun 11.30am–3pm, 5.30-11pm; €–€€
Seasonal French-inspired cuisine is served up in this luxuriously decorated restaurant, with various menu options as well as à la carte.

OSTEND

Leave the foreign tourists in Bruges and join the Belgians in the country's most popular seaside resort, reached in just 10 minutes by train from Bruges. It has a vast beach, fine seafood restaurants, museums and endless bustle.

British Connection

The British frequented Ostend en masse during its 19th-century heyday, arriving in ferries from Dover to play lawn tennis, golf and beach croquet. In the 1860s Britons numbered 2,000 out of the town's total population of 16,000. The English Church, founded in the 1780s, was consecrated in its current location on Langestraat in 1865, complete with royal pew for the occasions when Queen Victoria visited her uncle King Leopold I.

DISTANCE 5km (3 miles)
TIME A full day
START Museum Ship *Amandine*
END *Mercator*
POINTS TO NOTE

A combined train-and-bike ticket from Bruges will cover the return fare and bike hire from Ostend Station, a good option out of season when the promenades are empty and you want to whisk from one attraction to another. Trains to the coast get extremely busy on fine days and in holiday periods: arrive early to get a seat. The Tourist Office (*see p.80*) offers a City Pass valid for one year for entry to local museums and attractions, and represents a good saving if you plan to visit several paying sights.

---

see p.80

A former fortified town, Ostend transformed from a major fishing port to a chic holiday resort with the advent of the railways in the 19th century, when it was favoured by Belgian royalty and wealthy foreign tourists. War damage and the demands of modern tourism erased much of its *belle époque* charm, but recent efforts to restore its image are paying off. Its good train links, cultural life, lively shopping and restaurant scene make it one of the most popular places for day-trippers and holidaymakers.

MUSEUM SHIP *AMANDINE*

The green-hulled fishing trawler sunk in a dry dock opposite the railway station is the **Museum Ship** *Amandine* ❶ (Vindictivelaan 35; tel: 059 23 43 01; www.museum-amandine.be; daily 10am–5pm; charge). It's a fascinating evocation of life aboard a trawler, as experienced by generations of Ostend men on perilous voyages to abundant Arctic fishing grounds. Iceland eventually extended its territorial waters and put an end to their adventures; the *Amandine* was the last such trawler to be decommissioned, in 1995.

Food and Drink 🍴

① LE GRILLON

Visserskaai 31; tel: 059 70 60 63; www.legrillon.be; Fri–Tue noon–3pm, 6–10pm, Wed lunch only during hols; €€
Poached ray wing and other classics of the French seafood repertoire are prepared at this timeless classic by three superb chefs, one of whom has been at the helm for 40 years. The food and service are formal without being stuffy.

VISSERSKAAI

Walk up the quayside of **Fishermen's Wharf** (Visserskaai), a place of pilgrimage for its fish restaurants, seafood stalls and fish market. During the early morning trawlers dock along the quay and unload crates of ice-covered fish for restaurateurs and market traders. Herring gulls line the dock and seize any chance they get (beware the fines for anyone caught feeding them). Whether now or later, be sure to try a steaming whelk *(wullok)* soup from one of the stalls. Alternatively, have a leisurely dinner in one of the many good restaurants up here, such as **Le Grillon**, see ⑪①.

Fish Market

A little further up on the right, the utilitarian concrete block on the quayside houses the stalls of the **Fish Market** ❷ (Vistrap), open from 6 or 7am each day to sell the night's catch. Early birds

can watch as crates of sole, cod, haddock and halibut are winched up from fishing boats that dock alongside. Fish doesn't come fresher than this, although prices here are rather tourist-focused.

LANGESTRAAT

Turn left into Langestraat, which runs west to the casino. At no. 101 is the **English Church** *(see margin, opposite)*.

Museum of Local History

The first royal palace on the Belgian coast, at no. 69, is more bourgeois home than castle; it provides a fine setting for the **Ostend History Museum 'De Plate'** ❸ (Oostends Historisch Museum 'De Plate'; tel: 059 51 67 21; www.deplate.be; open Sat, hols and mid-June–mid-Sept except Tue 10am–noon and 2–5pm; charge). Inside 'the plaice' (as it is nicknamed) is a well-displayed collection of artefacts evoking the city's nautical past. There are model

Above from far left: fresh from the Fish Market; seafront.

Coastal Tram

The Coastal Tram (www.dekusttram.be) runs non-stop the length of the Belgian coast, linking De Panne by the French border with Knokke by the Netherlands, and passing through every resort on the way, often just metres behind the beach. Operated by Flemish public transport company De Lijn, the service runs from early morning to late at night, with tickets priced according to length of trip.

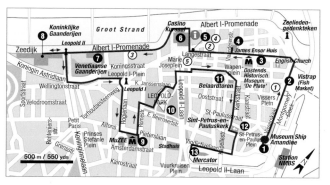

James Ensor

Belgo-Brit James Ensor (1860–1949) shifted from realism to paintings peopled with skeletons, masks and carnival figures. His style anticipated Expressionism by about 20 years and would give rise to the Surrealism of fellow Belgians René Magritte (1898–1971) and Paul Delvaux (1897–1994). The city still holds the Dead Rat Ball, a fundraising costume gala set up by Ensor and friends.

Below: seaside snaps.

yachts and liners, reconstructions of a fishermen's café and a living room of 1900, archaeological finds, historical maps tracing the changing shape of the city, photos and paintings depicting illustrious maritime events as well as daily life at the fish market, and colourful *belle époque* posters advertising cross-Channel ferry trips. Most curious of all is the preserved death-chamber of Belgium's first queen, Louise-Marie, wife of Leopold I, who died here of tuberculosis in 1850.

James Ensor House

At Vlaanderenstraat, turn right to visit, at no. 27, the **James Ensor House ❹** (James Ensor Huis; tel: 059 50 81 18; www.oostende.be; Wed–Mon 10am–noon and 2–5pm; charge). The painter was born in Ostend in 1860, and returned to live and work from 1916 until his death in 1949 above a modest souvenir shop run by his aunt and uncle. The shells, masks and curios in the shop's cabinets indicate where he may have sourced his inspiration. Upstairs, the original decor and furnishings of the living rooms have been restored. Reproductions of Ensor's artworks cover the walls, illustrating the fantastical imaginings of the artist *(see margin, left)*.

Casino Kursaal

Return to Langestraat, which has some of the liveliest watering holes in town, such as **Tao Bar**, see ⑪②. At its

western end is the **Tourist Office ❺** (Monacoplein 2; tel: 059 70 11 99; www.toerisme-oostende.be; Oct–May 10am–6pm, June–Sept 9am–7pm), where you can pick up a City Pass *(see box, p.78)*. Across the road is a proud Ostend institution – the **Casino Kursaal ❻**, a concert hall and casino with function rooms, bars and a chic restaurant on the top floor. In summer it also hosts club nights.

ALBERT I-PROMENADE

Walk around the casino and hit the promenade and main beach, having skipped a rather dull stretch of apartment blocks east of this point – the expanse of quartz sand dotted with traditional beach huts more than compensates. This is the place for pancake or ices on a terrace. Alternatively you could have something more substantial at **Beluga**, see ⑪③, or at family-run **Villa Borghese**, see ⑪④. For an idea of what was lost when most 19th-century seafront mansions were demolished, pause at the neo-Renaissance **Villa Maritza** at no. 76. Built in 1885, until recently it was an upmarket restaurant with a splendid view.

Royal Ostend

Further along the seafront are the 19th-century **Venetian Galleries ❼** (Venetiaanse Gaanderijen). At the entrance to this former royal pavilion stands a bronze sculpture, cast in 2000,

depicting the late **King Baudouin** (*r.*1951–93) on foot and wearing a raincoat on a visit to Ostend.

Albert I-Promenade melds into the Zeedijk (Sea Dyke). The equestrian statue on the left, created in 1931, depicts **King Leopold II** (*r.*1865–1909) gazing out to sea, flanked by Ostend fisherfolk and being hailed by a Congolese native. Given Leopold's brutish colonial rule over the Congo as well as his looting of its mineral wealth, the bare-faced cheek of this statue is astounding.

Continue to the colonnaded **Royal Galleries ❽** (Koninklijke Gaanderijen), built in 1906 so that Leopold II and his court could shelter from the wind as they passed along the seafront. The Art Deco **Thermae Palace Hotel** (www.thermaepalace.be) in the centre dates back to 1933.

Turn back to the Leopold statue and pass beneath the arch to reach Koningin Astridlaan. Turn left and walk via Warschauwstraat to Leopold I-Plein and its equestrian statue of **Leopold I** (*r.*1831–65), first King of the Belgians.

MUSEUM BY THE SEA

Head south on Rogierlaan and sidestep into Romestraat to reach the excellent **MuZEE ❾** (tel: 059 50 81 18; www.muzee.be; Tue–Sun 10am–6pm; charge). The Museum by the Sea (Kunstmuseum aan Zee) contains works by an impressive roster of Belgian artists: James Ensor, Leon Spilliaert, Paul Delvaux, Panamarenko, Jan Fabre as well as Luc Tuymans. It also hosts temporary exhibitions of international contemporary art, and the café does reasonably priced lunches and snacks.

Food and Drink

② TAO BAR
Langestraat 24–26; tel: 059 43 83 73; www.tao-oostende.be; restaurant: Wed–Sun 5.30–11.30pm, Sun and hols noon–2.30pm; bar: daily from 4pm, Wed, Sat and Sun from 2pm; €
This lounge, bar and fusion restaurant in the heart of the nightlife district is helping put the edge back into Ostend. The menu features Belgian, Thai, Mexican and tapas dishes, and then it's up on the dance floor for a dressed-up beach party with resident and guest DJs.

③ BELUGA
Kemmelbergstraat 33; tel: 059 51 15 88; www.beluga oostende.be; daily noon–3pm, 6–10pm; €€
Facing the promenade (despite its address), this restaurant is decorated in a hip marine style. It serves everything from warming onion soup to Belgian caviar, specialising particularly in Belgian produce. The service is friendly too.

④ VILLA BORGHESE
Van Iseghemlaan 65; tel: 059 80 40 32; Wed–Sun noon–2pm, 7–10pm; €
Cheery restaurant serving reliably tasty Italian fare. Pizzas, pastas and a range of Italian starters make up the lion's share of the menu. Warm service.

⑤ BRASSERIE DU PARC
Marie Joseplein 3; tel: 059 51 13 05; www.hotelduparc.be; daily from 8am; €
A beautiful Art Deco hotel-café with original fixtures and fittings and ageing intellectuals enjoying the paper and a cigarette – a gem in an otherwise post-war townscape. Breakfast and light brasserie meals are served in charmingly old-school style.

Above from left:
Ostend's marina; commemorating fallen soldiers at Ypres; World War I trenches at Hill 62.

LEOPOLDPARK

Walk north up Romestraat, cross Alfons Pieterslaan and up Leon Spilliaertstraat to the **Leopold Park** (Leopoldpark) ⑩, a landscaped park with a lake and bridges, a playground for under-10s, a mini-golf course and a pleasant café. Cross the park diagonally to exit at the northern corner on Leopold II-Laan. Continue up to Marie Joseplein, where you could pause for a drink in the stylish **Brasserie du Parc**, see ⑪⑤ *(p.81)*.

WAPENPLEIN

Turn right along Adolph Buylstraat, a pedestrianised street which leads to **Wapenplein** ⑪. This square, the geographical and commercial heart of the city, is dominated by the **Belltower** (Beiaardtoren), built in 1964, which plays a tune composed by James Ensor. The adjoining building (1958), once a museum of fine arts, is now a **shopping arcade**.

Below: Leopoldpark.

CHURCH OF SS PETER AND PAUL

Take Kerkstraat south (or, if you prefer to walk past shops, parallel Kapellestraat) to the neo-Gothic **Church of SS Peter and Paul** ⑫ (Sint-Petrus-en-Pauluskerk; Sint-Petrus-en-Paulusplein; tel: 059 80 04 27; daily; free). Completed in 1907 by Bruges architect Louis Delacenserie, it includes a chapel (behind the choir) for the mausoleum of Queen Louise-Marie, who died in Ostend in 1850. The lovely stained-glass windows were added after World War II. To the west is **Saint Peter's Tower** (St Pieterstoren; closed for works), the remainder of the first St Peter's church (1458). The octagonal tower was added in the early 18th century and explains its nickname, De Peperbus (The Peppermill).

MARINA

Exiting the church, take Dekenijstraat south to the yacht marina, home to the three-masted schooner *Mercator* ⑬ (Mercatordok; tel: 059 51 70 10; www.zeilschip-mercator.be; daily 10am–5pm except 24, 25 and 31 Dec and 1 Jan; charge). This former merchant navy training ship once sailed as far as Easter Island; its sumptuous polished wood furnishings are a far cry from the basic quarters aboard the *Amandine*, a short walk away.

YPRES

14

The history of Ypres (Ieper in Flemish) is one of glory and tragedy. One of the largest and richest cities of medieval Europe, it became a byword for the horrors of trench warfare during World War I, and was reconstructed from ruin after 1918.

Few visitors to the tranquil town of Ypres (Ieper) are aware that in 1260 it had a population that matched London's – 50,000-strong – and a reputation for weaving the finest cloth in Europe. Despite being part of France, the town sided with England during the Hundred Years War due to its dependence on English wool supplies. It backed the wrong horse – plague, starvation and battle ensued, and by the 15th century cloth production and the population had both declined by 90 percent.

A fortress town for the next four centuries, its ramparts proved useless against the shells of World War I, when it was blasted to oblivion as German and British forces dug into a line of trenches east of the city. Repeated offensives from 1914–18 claimed hundreds of thousands of lives, while the lines barely shifted. After the Armistice, the town was almost entirely rebuilt, complete with medieval monuments. The now affluent town has embraced its role as a place of pilgrimage for students of history and families of those who died on the Front.

DISTANCE Walk: 3km (2 miles); drive: 34km (21 miles)
TIME A full day
START/END Walk: Grote Markt; drive: Meenseweg beyond Menin Gate
POINTS TO NOTE
Ypres is 60km (37 miles) south-west of Bruges. Hourly trains connect Bruges to Ypres (at least 1½ hours; change at Kortrijk). By car the fastest route is via the A17/E403 south to Kortrijk, taking the Moorsele exit and travelling west on the A19 to Ieper (70km/43 miles; around 50 min). Two Bruges and several Ypres-based tour operators organise trips to the battlefields *(see margin, right)*, which are worth considering if you do not have your own transport and would like to visit out-of-town cemeteries. If possible, avoid the In Flanders Fields Museum on Tue, Thur and Fri during term-time, when many school groups visit.

Battlefield Tours
Tour operators Quasimodo (tel: 050 37 04 70; www. quasimodo.be) and Visit Bruges (free-phone in Belgium: 0800 99 133; tel from abroad: +32 (0)50 34 60 60; www.visit bruges.org) organise trips to Ypres from Bruges. Within Ypres, Flanders Battlefield Tours (tel: 057 36 04 60; www.ypres-fbt. be) and Over The Top Tours (tel: 057 33 29 00; www.overthetop tours-ypres.be) are just two of several local tour guides, which can tailor visits on request.

GROTE MARKT

From the railway station, the city centre
is about 1km (²/₃ mile) on foot. Cross the
road in front to Colaertplein, keeping
the garden to your left. Walk down
Stationstraat, turn left at the end on
Tempelstraat then right on Boterstraat.
Round the corner is **De Ruyffelaer**
⑪①, which is a great spot for a hearty
meal after a day's walking. But for now
continue along Boterstraat to the **Grote
Markt** ❶, the hub of activity in this otherwise tranquil town. Looking at the
buildings, from the immense Cloth Hall

and Belfry on your left to the individu-
ally designed houses, it is hard to grasp
that the entire square was rebuilt to its
medieval design after World War I. It
is now lined with restaurants and cafés,
including **Old Tom**, see ⑪②.

Cloth Hall
The vast **Cloth Hall** (Lakenhalle) bears
witness to Ypres's prominence as a
medieval wool town. (Bruges used to
have one.) Longer than the cathedral
(120m/394ft) and with 48 doors to the
street, it was originally built in
1250–1378 alongside the River Ieperlee
(now vaulted). Boats sailed into the
building, which served as a storehouse
and market for wool and cloth. Halfway
along sits the 70m (230ft) **Belfry**
(Belfort); a stump was all that remained
in 1918. Next door is the **Tourist Office**
(tel: 057 23 92 20; www.visitypres.be;
Apr–mid-Nov Mon–Sat 9am–6pm,
Sat–Sun 10am–6pm, mid-Nov–Mar
until 5pm), which has several exhibits.

In Flanders Fields Museum
The Cloth Hall's first floor houses the
excellent **In Flanders Fields Museum**
❷ (tel: 057 23 92 20; www.inflanders
fields.be; Apr–mid-Nov daily 10am–
6pm, mid-Nov–Mar 10am–5pm, last
entry 1hr before; closed early Jan;
charge). Named after the poem by
Canadian physician and poet John
McCrae (1872–1918), who died on
active service, the museum brings to life
the conflict that claimed 550,000 lives

on the Flemish front from 1914–18. Maquettes describe battles that took place for mere metres of territory over four years along the Ypres Salient; personal letters, mementoes and recordings evoke the human experience of trench warfare; and an audio soundscape recreates No Man's Land in chilling style.

ST MARTIN'S CATHEDRAL

Pass through the arch beneath the Belfry to reach **St Martin's Cathedral** ❸ (Sint-Maartenskathedraal; Vandepeereboomplein; daily 2–5pm, some mornings; free). Founded in the 11th century on the site of a fortified chapel of the counts of Flanders, the Gothic church was originally built in 1221. A bishopric from 1559–1801, the church was confiscated following the French Revolution and sold for building materials, but a churchwarden managed to buy it back. The current edifice was rebuilt 1922–30, when it gained a steeple of 102m (335ft). For refreshment nearby, try 't **Ganzeke**, see ⑪③.

ST GEORGE'S MEMORIAL CHURCH

At the northwestern corner of the square before the cathedral is the Anglican **St George's Memorial Church** ❹ (Apr–Sept daily 9.30am–8pm, Oct–Mar daily 9.30am–4.30pm), erected in memory of British and Commonwealth soldiers who died in World War I. Fur-

nished with donations from bereaved families, the personalised stained glass, banners, kneelers, pews and plaques make it a moving shrine to a sacrificed generation. An attached schoolhouse, funded by Eton School to honour old boys who had died, was opened for the children of War Graves Commission staff to teach them 'English and good manners'. Today, it is the church hall.

MENIN GATE

Return to the Grote Markt and cross to the southeastern corner, taking Meensestraat to the **Menenpoort** ❺ (Menin Gate), an arch inscribed with

Food and Drink

① DE RUYFFELAER
Gustave de Stuersstraat 9; tel: 057 36 60 06; www.deruyff elaer.be; Thur–Fri 5.30–10pm, Sat–Sun 11.30am–10pm; €
Much acclaimed restaurant, with a menu of traditional Flemish dishes (rabbit, pork belly, eel) following grandma's recipes with locally sourced ingredients. The restaurant's dark wood décor, floor tiles and open fire are reassuringly traditional.

② OLD TOM
Grote Markt 8; tel: 057 20 15 41; www.oldtom.be; Thur–Tue noon–2.30pm, 6–9.30pm (drinks 7.30am–11pm); €€
This hotel-bistro is favoured by the good burghers of Ypres and serves Belgian classics like shrimp croquettes, mussels and eels. Service can be slow when the terrace gets busy.

③ 'T GANZEKE
Vandepeereboomplein 5; tel: 057 20 00 09; Tue–Sun 9am–10.30pm, Fri–Sat until 11.30pm; €
This tavern and tearoom, decorated with model geese, serves a wide range of snacks and full meals round the clock. Tasty and affordable, whether for a pancake, soup or steak.

War Graves
The body responsible for maintaining Commonwealth war graves can be contacted for details of individual burial locations (www.cwgc.org).

the names of 55,000 of the 100,000 Commonwealth soldiers who died in battle before 16 August 1917 but have no known grave (those who perished later are commemorated in Tyne Cot cemetery; *see p.87*). Every evening at 8pm traffic through the gate is stopped and Ypres firefighters play 'The Last Post' on silver bugles to mark the city's gratitude to those who died fighting for Belgium's freedom and independence.

RAMPARTS

Climb the steps in the Menin Gate's southern side and walk south along the former city **ramparts**. Dating back to the 10th century, today they reflect the 17th-century layout created by French fortress designer Vauban for Louis XIV, providing a view of historic bastions, gates and islands. During World War I, sleeping quarters and hospitals were set up in tunnels within the ramparts (accessible only by guided tour).

Lille Gate and Ramparts Cemetery
Continue to **Lille Gate** ❻ (Rijselpoort), the oldest city gate, built under Burgundian rule in the 14th century. Just beyond, by the water, is the **Ramparts Cemetery** ❼, where the 193 Allied graves include members of the Maori Battalion, Canadian Engineers, Royal Irish Rifles and Essex Regiment. The impeccable lawn and flower-beds are a hallmark of the Commonwealth War Graves Commission *(see margin, left)*.

CITY MUSEUM

Turn back towards town and walk up Ieperleestraat, parallel to and west of busy Rijselsestraat. A rare historic building to have survived the 1914–18 bombardments, **St John's Almshouse** (Sint-Jansgodshuis) at no. 31 was an institution for the poor from 1270. Today, it houses the **City Museum** ❽ (Stedelijk Museum; Tue–Sun 10am–12.30pm, 2–6pm, Nov–Mar until 5pm; charge, or included in In Flanders Fields Museum ticket). Paintings from the 18th and 19th centuries illustrate the 'lost' Ypres, a film explains the city's turbulent past, and there's a focus on Louise De Hem (1866–1922), a local artist who braved social disapproval to pursue her career in a man's world.

To rejoin the Grote Markt, turn right twice and then left along Rijselsestraat.

Cat Parade

One of Belgium's more bizarre folkloric festivals takes place in Ypres every three years on the second Sunday in May (the next in 2015). The Kattenstoet (Cat Parade) recalls the medieval tradition of hurling live cats from the top of the Belfry to ward off evil spirits, a practice maintained until 1817 (and revived between the two world wars). The costumed procession of some 2,000 participants, horses, giants and ornate floats, evoke the symbolism of the cat in history and folklore. It culminates with the cat-throwing (soft toys only) and a witch-burning party. Seating is available at several points along the route; book in advance, through the tourist board.

Above from far left:
former city ramparts;
Tyne Cot Cemetery.

YPRES SALIENT

If you have your own transport, the following circuit visits principal World War I sites out of town. Take the road to Menen beyond the gate. Follow Zonnebeekseweg for a short distance, then turn right on Meenseweg (N8). After about 3km (2 miles), turn right on Canadalaan, where there are signs for Sanctuary Wood and Hill 62.

Sanctuary Wood and Hill 62

Sanctuary Wood Museum (Canadalaan 26; tel: 057 46 63 73; daily 10am–6pm; charge) is owned by the family of the original farmer. Its collection of armaments, shells, 3D photographs and uniforms is unlabelled, but the highlight, in a patch of adjoining woodland, is one of the few remaining sections of trench lines, surrounded by shell-holes.

Continue a short walk up the road to **Hill 62**, the Canadian memorial (62m/38ft above sea level) marking the site of fierce fighting in 1916 by Canadian troops defending the southern stretch of the Ypres Salient.

Passchendaele Museum

Return to the N8, turn left towards Ypres and then immediately right on narrow Begijnenbosstraat. This cuts the corner to reach the N37, where you should turn right towards Zonnebeke. At the centre in Zonnebeke Château is the **Memorial Museum Passchendaele 1917** (Feb–Nov daily 9am–5pm; tel: 051 77 04 41; www.passchendaele.be; charge), recounting the bloody Third Battle of Ypres in dioramas, photos and film, plus a reconstructed dugout.

Tyne Cot

Continue through Zonnebeke to the suburb of Broodseinde, turn left on the N303 for about 1km (²/₃ mile) and then left (follow signs) to **Tyne Cot Cemetery**, the world's largest Commonwealth cemetery. The most potent reminder of Passchendaele, it honours the victims of 100 days' fighting for a gain of barely 8km (5 miles): 245,000 British and 215,000 German troops. The **Visitor Centre** (Feb–Nov daily 10am–6pm) evokes their stories.

German Soldiers' Cemetery

Return to Zonnebeke and turn right at the roundabout. At the N313 turn right then immediately left to Langemark and right at the church. As you exit the village, the **German Soldiers' Cemetery** (Deutscher Soldatenfriedhof) is on the left, the only German war cemetery on the Ypres Salient. From the car park just beyond the cemetery, follow the audiovisual presentation on the path to the cemetery, a sombre place in pink sandstone and granite beneath oak trees. Buried here are 44,000 soldiers, many of them members of Student Regiments *(see margin, right)*. From Langemark, return to the N313, turning right for a straight run back to Ypres.

Student Massacre

Around 15 percent of Germany's volunteer corps raised at the outbreak of the war were students and high-school graduates, many recruited in entire classes with their professors. On 24 October 1914 the enthusiastic but untrained volunteers were sent marching at Langemark towards the only professional army in Europe, the British Expeditionary Force (BEF). They died in their thousands, prompting the Germans to remember the battle as the 'massacre of the innocents at Ypres' ('Kindermord bei Ypern').

GHENT

Vibrant, historic Ghent is 20 minutes by train from Bruges. While the city may lack the latter's picture-postcard prettiness, it does have at least as many sights and a lively urban edge thanks to a large student population.

DISTANCE 2.5km (1½ miles)
TIME A full day
START St Nicholas Church
END St Michael's Church
POINTS TO NOTE

As in Bruges, most museums in Ghent close on a Monday. However, the two big sights, St Bavo's and the Castle of the Counts, do open then. There are two trains hourly from Bruges to Gent-Sint-Pieters Station. Upon arrival, head to the tram stop under the bridge to the left as you exit the station and take tram no. 1 to Korenmarkt in the centre. Avoid walking, as the route is long and uninteresting. If coming by car, take the E40.

Below: enjoying outdoor drinks on Sint-Baafsplein.

Over twice the size of Bruges and with more dispersed sites, Ghent, on the confluence of the Leie and Scheldt rivers, grew rich on its cloth industry and the import of grain, and was prized by the counts of Flanders and dukes of Burgundy. This circuit concentrates on the historic centre, where there is plenty to see within a small radius, including one of the finest paintings in Western art,

the van Eyck altarpiece, in the cathedral. A longer visit can be rewarding, as Ghent has two fine art museums towards its periphery and a lively cultural scene. The youthful demographic means the city has many more budget options for dining out than in Bruges and some seriously good nightlife.

ST NICHOLAS CHURCH

Alight from the tram at Korenmarkt and **St Nicholas Church** ❶ (Sint-Niklaaskerk; www.stniklaas.com; Mon 2–5pm, Tue–Sun 10am–5pm; free). The 13th-century church in Scheldt Gothic style was founded by the city's Tradesmen's Guild. It suffered centuries of neglect, starting with stability problems in the 16th century, yet has survived repeated calls for demolition. Works begun in 1957 have reached the nave; the transept, choir and ambulatory are open and have been restored to their Gothic austerity – unlike the Baroque altar and other decoration added in the 17th century when the western portal was built (visible from outside). Properties built against the church's northern facade on Klein Turkije give an idea of how the entire exterior used to appear.

BELFRY

Walk east from St Nicholas to Sint-Baafsplein, where church and city authorities faced each other across the square. The **Belfry ❷** (Belfort; www.visitgent.be; daily 10am–6pm; charge) was completed in 1380 following the guilds' entry onto the town council. The tower, at 91m (299ft) tall, was intended as a symbol of the guilds' power – the charter detailing the rights and privileges of the people was stored in a strongroom here, while the bells took over from churches the task of informing citizens at what time to get up and go to work. Originally, there was just one large bell (the Roeland bell from 1377), which rang hourly; a smaller chiming set was added later. The melody of the quarter-hourly chime is changed every two years just before Easter Sunday. Although less impressive to climb than the belfry in Bruges, at least this one has a lift. A guided tour is available in Dutch and English every day at 3.30pm.

Cloth Hall

Ghent, like Bruges, made its fortune from weaving cloth, which was valued, examined and sold in the 1441 **Cloth Hall** (Lakenhalle; *see margin, right*) next to the Belfry. The **Tourist Office** (09 266 56 60; www.visitgent.be; mid-Mar–mid-Oct 9.30am–6.30pm, rest of year until 4.30pm) is situated in the crypt, but the main building may not be visited.

ST BAVO'S CATHEDRAL

Facing the Belfry on the eastern side of Sint-Baafsplein is **St Bavo's Cathedral ❸** (Sint-Baafskathedraal; Apr–Oct Mon–Sat 8am–6pm, Sun 1–6pm, Nov–Mar until 5pm, Sun 1–5pm; http://users.skynet.be/sintbaafskathedraal-gent; free). A mix of sombre high Gothic and flamboyant late Gothic style, built during the 14th–16th centuries, the church started out as plain St John's, founded in the 10th century and the first parish church in Ghent. In 1559 it gained cathedral status and a dedication to the 7th-century Flemish saint St Bavo. The cavernous interior is rich in treasures, most notably the

Above from far left: Graslei; detail from St Bavo's Cathedral.

The Suckler

An annexe (1741) to the Cloth Hall's western facade was used as the guard's quarters when the hall served as a jail. This is known as The Suckler (De Mammelokker), after the sculpture above the doorway showing Roman Charity: Cimon being suckled by his daughter Pero, a wet-nurse.

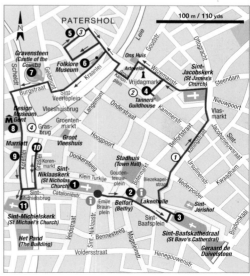

Above from left:
St Bavo's Cathedral;
The Adoration of the Mystic Lamb.

Mystic Lamb altarpiece. Other highlights include the Rubens altarpiece (1624), in which the artist portrays himself as St Bavo, and Frans Pourbus the Elder's *Jesus among the Scribes* (1571), the cast of which includes Emperor Charles V, his son King Philip II of Spain and the artist Pieter Brueghel the Elder. The Baroque high altar (1719) is a triumph of pomp in white, black and red-flamed marble, while the Baroque organ (1653) is the largest in Benelux, with 7,000 pipes. Among many other artworks, the series of bishop portraits from the 16th century to the present makes for a fascinating study of ecclesiastical fashions.

Mystic Lamb

Belgium's greatest art treasure alone justifies the trip to Ghent: *The Adoration of the Mystic Lamb* (1432), or the Ghent Altarpiece, by Jan and Hubert van Eyck *(see feature)*. The 20-panel polyptych marked a turning point for painting and religious art, blending Gothic ideals of abstraction and mysticism with the realism and naturalism that characterised the Renaissance. Although designed for the cathedral's Vijdt chapel (beyond the high altar), it is displayed in the **former baptismal chapel** (Mon–Sat 9.30am–5pm, Sun and hols 1–5pm, Nov–Mar 10.30am–4pm; charge), to the left of the door as you enter.

The altarpiece was commissioned by wealthy alderman Judocus Vijdt and his wife; their portraits appear on the back panels of the closed polyptych. The childless couple chose the Annunciation theme, and the artist included esoteric symbols that would have been appreciated by the patron and Philip the Good, duke of Burgundy. Among the 200 figures depicted, there are references to Virgil, Jewish texts, Byzantium and science. One panel – the 'Just Judges', on the lower left – was stolen in 1934 and a ransom note sent to the bishop. It has never been recovered.

Brothers van Eyck

The *Mystic Lamb* altarpiece is attributed to brothers Hubert and Jan van Eyck, but much debate surrounds the role of each artist. A note in Latin on the panel indicates that the panel was largely the work of Hubert, 'the greatest artist ever known', and completed after his death in 1426 by Jan, his junior by 20 years and 'second in art', according to the inscription. Hubert, an illuminator of whom only one other work survives, is thought to have taught Jan the technique of oil painting, elaborating a formula that was kept secret from Italian painters until the end of the 15th century. But Jan would surpass Hubert in stature and fame and, as a result, many later commentators have questioned Hubert's contribution and credit Jan alone for the work.

VRIJDAGMARKT

Exit St Bavo's and take narrow Biezekapelstraat to your right. Cross Hoogpoort and continue down Zandberg. For a wholesome lunch here, try **De Warempel**, see ⑪①.

Head straight on, then turn left at the end to face **St James's Church** (Sint-Jacobskerk; *see margin, right*). Walk around the church and straight on to reach **Vrijdagmarkt** ❹, named after the Friday market held here since the 13th century. Bordered by guildhouses and mansions, the square has been the scene of jousting tournaments, executions and political skirmishes; now bordered by cafés, it is liveliest at night. **Dulle Griet** has the best beer selection, see ⑪②.

Jacob van Artevelde Statue
The bronze **statue** (1863) at the centre of the square commemorates textiles merchant and brewer Jacob van Arte-velde (*c.*1290–1345), who in 1338, during the Hundred Years War between France and England, rallied Ghent's merchants and guilds in support of England's King Edward III against the count of Flanders. Seven years later, he was assassinated on Vrijdagmarkt during a riot between weavers and wool-makers after suggesting that Edward the Black Prince, son of Edward III, should be made count of Flanders.

Guildhouses
The square's most striking house is the **Tanners' Guildhouse** (Gildehuis van de Huidevetters) on the corner of Kam-merstraat. Built 1450–83, it was the meeting place for the weavers' quality commission, who would shame poor-quality work by hanging bolts of linen or cloth from its Little Tower (Toreken).

Socialist Headquarters
On the opposite side of the square, the Art Nouveau edifice **Our House** (Ons Huis) was the headquarters of the Socialist workers' association, built in 1899. Its gold inscription, in Dutch, reads 'Workers of World Unite'.

PATERSHOL DISTRICT

Leave Vrijdagmarkt via Grootkanon-plein and cross the bridge. The streets behind Kraanlei quayside form **Pater-shol** ❺, where recent renovation has transformed this former red-light district of 17th-century houses into a hip quarter with boutiques, bars and restaurants, including the exclusive **De Blauwe Zalm**, see ⑪③ *(p.93)*. The city has made a keen effort to pre-serve the residential character of the

Street Festival
For 10 days in mid-July, Gentenaars hold one of Europe's largest music, theatre and street festivals, the Ghent Festivities (Gentse Feesten). Centred around St James's Church (Sint-Jacobskerk), events include a re-enactment of the Noose Bearers' (Stroppendragers) Procession, recalling the humiliation of rebellious citizens by Charles V in 1540.

Food and Drink 🍴

① DE WAREMPEL
Zandberg 8; tel: 09 224 30 62; Mon–Fri except hols 11.45am–2pm; €
The menu at this vegetarian lunch restaurant and local favourite comprises a one-dish mixed platter, with optional soup starter and dessert. The custom, if you do not book, is to join a table with other diners.

② DULLE GRIET
Vrijdagmarkt 50; tel: 09 224 24 55; www.dullegriet.be; Mon 4.30pm–1am, Tue–Sat noon–1am, Sun noon–7.30pm; €
Behind the lace lampshades and café curtains, this old-style Flemish tavern serves 250 different beers, including Ghent's own Stropken, Gentse Tripel and Augustijnerbier, and the renowned Kwak (served in a 1.5 litre glass, for which a shoe is required as deposit).

The Alijn Reparation

The Huis van Alijn almshouse was founded in 1363 in reparation for a family feud. In 1354 a girl named Godelieve chose to marry Hendrik Alijn instead of her intended, Simeon Rijm. In revenge, Rijm killed Alijn and his brother. As punishment, the Rijm family homes were demolished, and Simeon was ordered to build an almshouse on land donated by the Alijns. The original was replaced in 1519.

Below: inside the Design Museum.

neighbourhood, which was once home to tanners and weavers, and there are strict rules regulating the number of businesses here.

Folklore Museum

Walk south down Kraanlei to no. 65, the **Folkore Museum** ❻ (Huis van Alijn; tel: 09 269 23 50; www.huis vanalijn.be; Tue–Sat 11am–5pm, Sun 10am–5pm; charge). Located in a former children's hospital *(see margin, left)*, it displays a collection of artefacts pertaining to birth, illness, marriage and death rituals, the evolution of leisure time, and traditional crafts and trades. A projection room showing 'found footage' from home movies, and a 'speaking chamber', with recordings of the various Flemish dialects, are both fascinating.

CASTLE OF THE COUNTS

At the end of Kraanlei, turn right to Sint-Veerleplein and the **Castle of the Counts** ❼ (Gravensteen; tel: 09 225 93 06; www.visitgent.be; daily Apr–Sept 10am–6pm, Oct–Mar 9am–5pm; charge). Built by the counts of Flanders in the 11th century, the castle was used, successively, as a fortress, administrative centre and court of justice (14th–18th centuries), and factory and workers' residence (19th century). The visit to the battlements and keep culminates in a room containing gruesome torture instruments.

DESIGN MUSEUM

Walk west, cross the bridge, then turn south into Jan Breydelstraat. At no. 5, the Hotel De Coninck houses the **Design Museum Gent** ❽ (tel: 09 267 99 99; www.designmuseumgent.be; Tue–Sun 10am–6pm; charge), with 17th- and 18th-century furniture in the front house and a superb Art Nouveau collection in the modern wing, plus furniture from the 1970s and 80s. Built in 1755, the former family mansion was furnished in the height of luxury before its owner's wedding. The panelled dining-room is original, embellished with motifs to love and marriage, with an ornate Baroque chandelier in carved oak. After so much visual stimulus, the **Brooderie** bakery-café opposite will be a welcome stop, see ⑪④.

KORENLEI AND GRASLEI

Jan Breydelstraat brings you to the city's commercial centre during the 11th–18th centuries. The stretch of the River Leie known as 'Tussen Bruggen' (Between the Bridges) formed a harbour, flanked with guildhouses and warehouses. Many buildings here were renovated for the 1913 Ghent World Fair, not always with great attention to historical accuracy, but the effect is still stunning; the broad quaysides still buzz with activity on a fine day, although beer-drinking students have replaced haggling merchants.

On the western bank is **Korenlei** ❾ (Grass Quay), with the renovated 16th-century **The Swan** (De Swane) at no. 9. The former brewery is now a Marriott hotel. At no. 7, the **Guildhouse of the Tied Boatmen**, known as The Anchor (Den Ancker), was built in 1739. Tied Boatmen were not permitted to unload their cargo within the city limits, and had to tranship their loads onto the vessels of the Free Boatmen *(see below)*.

On **Graslei** ❿ (Herb Quay), opposite, the late-12th-century Romanesque **Corn Stockpile House** (Het Spijker) at no. 9 was used to store grain until 1734. Its Tournai limestone facade contains what is thought to be the oldest step gable in the country. Next door, at no. 11, is the Flemish Renaissance **Little Customs House** (Tolhuisje), where duties were paid on grain stored. Nos 12–13 were the **Corn Measurer's House** (Korenmetershuis or Coorenmetershuys), a Gothic building from 1540 with Baroque gable (1698). No. 14 is the **Guildhouse of the Free Boatmen** (Gildenhuis van de Vrije Schippers), built in 1355 with a facade from 1531.

ST MICHAEL'S CHURCH

Graslei brings you to **St Michael's Bridge** (1910), with fine views north over the river and east to Ghent's three great towers. To the west of the bridge stands **St Michael's Church** ⓫ (Sint-Michielskerk; Apr–Sept Mon–Sat 2–5pm; free), which was commissioned by the Brewers' Guild in 1440, but never got a tower due to lack of funds. Inside, the space seems immense, with many side chapels. Artworks include *Christ on the Cross* (1630) by Anthony van Dyck.

Food and Drink

③ **DE BLAUWE ZALM**
Vrouwebroersstraat 2; tel: 09 224 08 52; www.deblauwezalm.be; closed Sat and Mon lunch, and all Sun; €€€
A must for gastronomes, the 'Blue Salmon' is renowned for inventive fish and seafood. Instead of formulaic standards, its concoctions use local specialities like asparagus, oriental spices or Mediterranean herbs, served in a stylish modern interior or garden terrace.

④ **BROODERIE**
Jan Breydelstraat 8; tel: 09 225 06 23; www.brooderie.be; Tue–Sun 8am–6pm; €
Breakfast, lunch and afternoon teas are served on scrubbed pine tables in this homely bakery store, which also has B&B rooms upstairs. Cakes are homemade and portions are generous: the moist, dark spice cake is a local speciality.

DIRECTORY

A user-friendly alphabetical listing of practical information, plus hand-picked hotels and restaurants, clearly organised by area, to suit all budgets and tastes. Select nightlife listings are also included here.

A

AGE RESTRICTIONS

The age of consent in Belgium is 16. The legal minimum driving age using a full licence is 18. The legal drinking age in bars is 16, or 18 for distilled and strong spirits. There is no minimum legal age for buying alcohol, except for spirits, where the legal age is 18.

B

BUDGETING

Average costs in euros (€):

Glass of beer or house wine: €5

Main course at a restaurant: budget €13; moderate €22; expensive €30

Room for two including breakfast: cheap hotel: €60; moderate hotel: €110; deluxe hotel: €180

Single bus ticket: €1.60

Museum pass: provides entry to all city museums over three days for €15, or a year's pass costs €25.

Brugge City Card: an access-all-areas pass to the city's top sights (www.brugge citycard.be) is €35 for 48 hours or €40 for 72 hours and includes entry to 23 museums and other paying attractions, a free canal boat tour between March and mid-November, and minimum 25 percent discounts on other things such as cultural events and bike hire. It can be purchased online, or in Bruges from the Tourist Office, hotels or city vendors.

C

CHILDREN

Bruges is a safe and child-friendly destination. Traffic is very light and the city is compact and easy to navigate on foot, making it much less tiring to visit than many city destinations. The canals and bridges add to its appeal, and there are several parks with playgrounds. Further afield are numerous attractions such as country parks and the coast, less than a quarter of an hour away by train.

Entrance to city-owned museums (including the Belfry, Groeninge, Folklore, etc) is free for children under 13. For most other attractions, children pay a reduced price or enter for free if young.

Most hotels will have family rooms or be able to provide a child's bed on request. Check in advance for availability. The more upscale hotels can also arrange babysitting, if required. Alternatively, contact the Flemish government childcare agency Kind en Gezin for a list of approved babysitters (tel: 050 44 65 50; email: info@kindengezin.be).

CLOTHING

Weather can be changeable in Bruges, as it is just 12km (7 miles) from the North Sea coast and has a maritime climate *(see p.12)*. Light layers of clothing are most suitable in late spring to early autumn, with rainproof and warm layers for evenings. In winter, although snow

is rare, icy winds sweep over the polders from the north and east, and a warm coat with hat, scarf and gloves are advisable. Belgians tend to prefer a discreet, smart-casual style, but all styles are tolerated. Above all, wear comfortable shoes suitable for walking on cobbled streets; avoid stilettos.

CRIME AND SAFETY

Crime is not a worry in Bruges, although you cannot entirely rule it out. As in any popular tourist area, keep an eye on your belongings. If you arrive via Brussels, be particularly vigilant in Brussels Gare du Midi station, where thieves and pick-pockets are active. Bagsnatching is also common in international trains, especially between Brussels and Paris and Amsterdam. Thieves often work in teams of two or three and try to distract victims by asking questions, spilling food or drink, or telling travellers they have spilled something on their clothes.

CUSTOMS

There are no import limitations between EU countries as long as the goods are for personal use. Over-18s can import: 800 cigarettes, 400 cigarillos, 200 cigars, 1kg tobacco; 10 litres spirits, 20 litres fortified wine, 90 litres wine (or 60 litres sparkling) and 110 litres beer.

People arriving from non-EU countries may bring a maximum of 1l

spirits, 4l wine, 16l beer and 200 cigarettes or 50 cigars or 250g of tobacco, without paying value added tax or customs duties.

When shopping in Belgium, airport shops offer tax-free prices for people travelling to a non-EU country.

Anyone entering or leaving the EU will have to declare if they are carrying cash amounting to more than €10,000, or equivalent in other currencies.

D

DISABLED TRAVELLERS

Bruges is not particularly accessible due to its historic character; the narrow and cobbled streets can inhibit wheelchair use. Suitable accommodation should be booked well in advance. However, many museums have disabled access, while help with train travel can be arranged at stations, or contact the Tourist Office.

The Accessible Travel Info Point is an organisation set up by the Flemish Tourist Board to provide information for travellers with disabilities. See www.toegankelijkreizen.be.

E

ELECTRICITY

Electrical voltage in Belgium is 220 volts at 50 Hz. Plugs are round two-pin types. Adaptor plugs can be purchased at the airport or in hardware stores.

Above from far left: popular Belgian beer; touring the Dijver canal.

EMBASSIES AND CONSULATES

Australia: Rue Guimard 6, 1040 Brussels; tel: 02 286 05 00

Canada: Avenue de Tervuren 2, 1040 Brussels; tel: 02 741 06 11

New Zealand: Avenue des Nervien 9-31, 1000 Brussels; tel: 02 512 1040

Republic of Ireland: Chaussée d'Etterbeek 180, 1050 Brussels; tel: 02 282 34 00

South Africa: Rue Montoyer 17, 1040 Brussels; tel: 02 285 44 00

UK: Avenue d'Auderghem 10, 1040 Brussels; tel: 02 287 62 11

US: Boulevard du Régent 27, 1000 Brussels; tel: 02 811 40 00

EMERGENCIES

Ambulance, Fire: 100

Police: 101

General emergency number: 112

You can also call the Bruges police on 050 44 88 44 or visit the station at Lodewijk Coiseaukaai 2, just outside the perimeter canal in the north of the city.

ETIQUETTE

Belgians greet each other by shaking hands or kissing on the cheek. In more formal situations or with people you do not know, shake hands. Close acquaintances will kiss each other once, or to mark a special occasion or after a long absence three times on alternate cheeks; but never twice. The exception is in Brussels, where expats have adopted the French-style two-kiss greeting. Men sometimes kiss each other if they are of the same family or long-standing close friends.

If you are invited as a guest to the home of a Belgian, take flowers or good-quality chocolates as a gift to the hostess. Wine or spirits should only be given to close friends.

F

FURTHER READING

Bruges-la-Morte (1892) by Georges Rodenbach. Key Symbolist work in which the city embodies the grief of a widower who roams Bruges's streets.

The Sorrow of Belgium (1983) by Hugo Claus. This epic coming-of-age novel set in World War Two Flanders is an unflattering but vital portrait for anyone keen to understand modern Belgium.

The Lion of Flanders (1838) by Hendrik Conscience. A romantic 19th-century retelling of the Bruges-inspired revolt against the French in 1302.

The Legend of the Glorious Adventures of Tyl Ulenspiegel in the Land of Flanders & Elsewhere (1867) by Charles de Coster. Stories from medieval myths and legends are combined in this tale of a legendary folk hero, artist and prankster who, in this version, embodies the Flemish spirit and its resistance of Spanish occupation in the 16th century.

G

GAY/LESBIAN VISITORS

Belgium is a very gay-friendly country. It was the second country in the world (after the Netherlands) to legalise same-sex marriage, in January 2003. In 2006, gay couples gained the same rights as heterosexuals to adopt children. Bruges is not known for having a large gay community and certainly has a discreet party scene, but it is a very tolerant place and most venues are gay-friendly.

The website www.gaybruges.be lists social events and the addresses of restaurants, bars and hotels where gay folk are especially welcome, as well as the contacts required to organise a gay wedding.

GREEN ISSUES

Bruges has an enviable environmental situation. Refreshed by North Sea winds and encircled by grassy fields reclaimed from the sea centuries ago for farmland, it is a model of sustainable town planning, served by excellent public transport and flat enough to encourage anyone to hop on a bike. The only serious threats to the environment are to be found on the outskirts of the city and around Zeebrugge port, where development pressure has provoked fierce protest and the creation of a militant 'green belt' movement.

The city's canals have been cleaned up in recent decades; private boats are forbidden and fish have returned. The Flemish region claims to be the world champion of recycling: over 70 percent of domestic waste is separated for recycling. The public transport network is exemplary, here and throughout densely populated Belgium: buses serve the tiniest villages and the entire coastal strip is connected by an efficient tram service, which connects with trains to all cities. Generous public subsidies for renewable energy and public transport passes have also proved successful in changing public attitudes.

Carbon-Offsetting

Air travel produces a huge amount of carbon dioxide and is a significant contributor to global warming. If you would like to offset the damage caused to the environment by your flight, a number of organisations can do this for you, using online 'carbon calculators', which tell you how much to donate. In the UK travellers can visit www.climatecare.org or www.carbonneutral.com; in the US go to www.climatefriendly.com or www.sustainabletravelinternational.org.

H

HEALTH

Healthcare and Insurance

EU Nationals who fall ill in Belgium are eligible to receive emergency treatment. You will have to pay, but are entitled to claim back 75 percent of the

cost of seeing a doctor or dentist and of prescription drugs. You will have to pay part of the costs of hospital treatment. Ambulance travel is not covered.

To receive a refund you need a European Health Insurance Card. For UK citizens, these are available online at www.dh.gov.uk, by picking up an application form in a post office or call: 0845 606 2030. Irish citizens should visit www.ehic.ie. Reimbursements are handled in Belgium by Sickness Funds Offices (Mutualité/Ziekenfonds).

Non-EU citizens are advised to take out medical insurance before travelling.

The following non-profit group also offers members fixed rates for medical treatment abroad: International Association for Medical Assistance to Travellers (IAMAT), 40 Regal Road, Guelph, Ontario, N1K 1B5, Canada; tel: 519 836 0102; www.iamat.org. Members receive a medical record completed by their doctor and a directory of English-speaking IAMAT doctors on call 24 hours a day. Membership is free but donations are appreciated.

Pharmacies and Hospitals

Pharmacies are identifiable by a green neon cross sign. Most are open 9am–6.30pm. All pharmacies display in their window details of pharmacies *(apotheek)* that are on duty at night and weekends, or call 0900 10 500 (8.30–10pm) or 050 44 88 44 (10pm–9am).

The main Bruges hospital (including for A&E) is AZ Sint-Jan, Ruddershove 10; tel: 050 45 21 11; www.azbrugge.be

Telemedicine

The non-profit organisation Health Care Belgium was set up in 2007 to promote Belgium as a centre of medical excellence and encourage the delivery of medical services to foreign patients in an ethical and coordinated way. See www.healthcarebelgium.com.

HOURS AND HOLIDAYS

The standard business hours in Belgium are 8am–5pm or 9am–6pm. Shops usually open at 10am, sometimes closing for lunch. Banks close at 4pm and over the weekend. Most museums are closed on Mondays; shops are closed on Sundays and many on Mondays too, although in tourist destinations such as Bruges and the coastal resorts many stay open.

INTERNET FACILITIES

Internet cafés are not widely visible in Bruges as most residents have fast broadband at home and the city is not a major student or backpacker destination. Many hotels offer email facilities, although they may charge a high price for the service. Youth hostels offer an alternative; two are included below:

Bauhaus, Langestraat 135; tel: 050 34 10 93; www.bauhaus.be
Snuffel Sleep-In, Ezelstraat 47–49; tel: 050 33 31 33; www.snuffel.be
Teleboetiek, corner of Langestraat-Predikherenstraat; tel: 050 34 74 72

L

LANGUAGE

The language of Flanders is Dutch, or, correctly, 'Netherlandic'. Belgium has three official languages: Dutch (spoken by 58 percent of the population), French (31 percent, including a majority in Brussels) and German (11 percent), although English is widely spoken.

Useful Phrases
yes *ja*
no *nee*
please *alstublieft*
thank you (very much) *dank u (wel)*
excuse me *excuseer/pardon*
you're welcome *graag gedaan*
hello *dag/hallo*
goodbye *dag/tot ziens*
good morning *goedemorgen*
good afternoon *goedemiddag*
good evening *goedenavond*
Do you speak English? *Spreekt u Engels?*
I don't understand. *Ik begrijp het niet.*
I'm sorry. *Het spijt me./Sorry.*
I don't know. *Ik weet het niet.*
No problem. *Geen probleem.*

Can you help me? *Kunt u mij helpen?*
What is your name? *Hoe heet u?*
My name is… *Ik heet…*
How much is it? *Hoeveel is/kost het?*
Can I have…? *Mag ik hebben…?*
I am looking for… *Ik zoek… naar*
What do you recommend? *Wat beveelt u aan?*
I'd like… *Ik wil/zou graag…*

LEFT LUGGAGE

The railway station in Bruges has lockers and a staffed facility for left luggage. Opening hours are daily 6am–9.30pm.

LOST PROPERTY

For property lost on a train or in a station, see www.b-rail.be/nat/E/practical/lostobjects/index.php. The form is available in French or Dutch. Or call Bruges station lost property on 050 30 23 28.

If you lose your passport, contact your embassy or consulate to arrange temporary travel documents. For other lost items, contact the police, *see p. 98*.

M

MAPS

You will not normally need a map other than the one provided in this book. However, if you plan to travel outside the city by public transport, pick up a De Lijn map from the booth by the railway

station or the Tourist Office on 't Zand. Detailed topographical maps of Belgium are published by the National Geographic Institute, see: www.ngi.be

MEDIA

Print Media

Media ownership is largely in Belgian hands and highly concentrated into Flemish- and French-language press. There are numerous national and local newspapers; the main Flemish ones are *De Standaard* (quality, centre right), *De Morgen* (quality, centre left) and *Het Laatste Nieuws* (tabloid). The national news agency is Belga.

Radio

The Flemish public service broadcaster VRT (www.vrt.be) has the largest audience share in the Dutch-speaking north of Belgium. Its main stations are Radio 1 (news, talk and gameshows), Radio 2 (mainstream music), Klara (classical) and Studio Brussel (rock and alternative). The big commercial stations are Nostalgie (classic rock), Q Music (pop and rock) and Radio Contact.

Television

Over 90 percent of Belgian households have cable TV, which shows Belgian public and commercial channels as well as public television from France, the Netherlands, Germany and the UK. CNN, BBC World, MTV, Eurosport and CNBC are widely available. Digital TV has been slow to take off in Belgium due to the preponderance of cable.

English–Language Publications

Ackroyd Publications produces *The Bulletin*, which covers news, arts and lifestyle in Belgium, especially Brussels, and runs website www.xpats.com for the international community in Belgium.

MONEY

Currency

Belgium uses euros (€), divided into 100 cents. Banknotes come in 5, 10, 20, 50, 100, 200 and 500 euros.

Credit Cards

All major cards are accepted (Visa, MasterCard, Maestro, American Express and Diners Club). Most shops, restaurants and hotels accept credit cards, but few cafés or bars do.

Cash Machines

There are plenty of ATMs in the city and most take credit cards. Those which are contained within a bank's entrance porch are accessible during bank opening hours only, unless you have a Belgian Bancontact-Mister Cash card.

Traveller's Cheques

Traveller's cheques are widely accepted.

Tipping

Service charges and taxes are always included in prices. However, many

people round up the bill in a café or restaurant (especially if they are in a group) to show appreciation, usually between €0.5–3. Suggested tip for porter service is €1 per item, cloak-room attendants €1.25–2.50 per coat. Most public toilets require a tip to the attendants of 25–50 cents.

Taxes

Belgian VAT (21 percent, or 6 percent in certain sectors) is included in prices.

P

POST

The Belgian post office (De Post/La Poste) is nationalised and efficient, although thefts from packages are not uncommon. Mailboxes are red. Buy stamps from post offices and shops selling postcards. The cost of sending a regular-size postcard or letter weighing no more than 50g is €1.09 within Europe or €1.29 to other countries.

The main Bruges Post Office is on the Markt: Markt 5; tel: 022 01 23 45; www.post.be; Mon–Fri 9am–6pm, Sat 9am–3pm.

PUBLIC HOLIDAYS

1 January New Year's Day
1 May Labour Day
21 July National Day
15 August Assumption
1 November All Saints' Day
11 November Armistice Day
25 December Christmas Day
Movable dates: **Easter** (varying), **Easter Monday** (1st Monday after Easter), **Ascension** (6th Thursday after Easter), **Pentecost** (7th Sunday after Easter) and **Pentecost Monday** (8th Monday after Easter). Holidays falling on a weekend are taken the following Monday.

R

RELIGION

Belgium is a strong defender of religious freedom. Most Belgians are Roman Catholic (60 percent, but just 15 percent practising), but five other religions are recognised by the state: Protestantism, Islam, Orthodox, Judaism and Anglicanism. The federal government pays wages to their ministers. Religious or 'moral' teaching is obligatory in schools; children are instructed according to their choice in any of the six recognised religions or in non-religious ethics.

S

SMOKING

Smoking is banned in restaurants and bars, though bars may provide a separate smoking area. Smoking is forbidden on public transport, in enclosed public spaces and in most workplaces, although smoking rooms are often provided.

T

TELEPHONES

Fixed-line telephone numbers in Bruges start 050. You need to use the area code. The code for Belgium is +32. When dialling from abroad, omit the first 0 of the code. For English-speaking directory enquiries, tel: 1405. For online information: www.infobel.be

Prepaid calling cards can offer a substantial saving on standard rates and can be used from a fixed phone, pay phone or mobile phone. Cards are widely available, including in train stations, newspaper stands and supermarkets.

To make an international call, dial 00, followed by the country code (Australia +61, Canada +1, Ireland +353, UK +44, US +1), then the area code and number.

Mobile (Cell) Phones

If you come from North America, you will not be able to use your phone if it is a single-band device. If you have an unlocked dual-band GSM cell phone, you can buy a prepaid SIM card locally to avoid roaming charges. The three main mobile phone operators in Belgium are Proximus, Mobistar and Base.

TIME ZONES

Belgium is GMT+1 hour (+2 Apr–end Oct). When it is noon in Bruges, it is 11am in London, 6am in New York, 10pm in Sydney.

TOILETS

Public toilets are not widely available in Bruges: there are toilets at the station and by the Minnewater in the park. Some cafés charge for using the toilet, so non-patrons are free to use them too.

TOURIST INFORMATION

Toerisme Brugge, the tourist information service, is helpful and efficient. Staff are fluent in English. The tourist information bureau In&Uit is on the ground floor of the Concert Hall, 't Zand 34; tel: 050 44 46 46; www.bruges.be/toerisme; daily 10am–6pm.

Outside the country, contact the Flemish or Belgian tourist office:
UK: Tourism Flanders-Brussels, Flanders House, 1a Cavendish Square, London W1G OLD; tel: 020 7307 7730; www.visit-flanders.co.uk
US: Belgian Tourist Office, 220 East 42nd Street, Suite 3402 New York, NY 10017; tel: 212 758 8130; www.visit-belgium.com

TOURS AND GUIDES

Bike Tours

Quasimundo bike tours run Mar–Oct, 9.50am, starting at Toyo Ito pavilion on the Burg (reservation required). Knowledgeable and entertaining guides lead bike tours of the city. Children under 8 free (Nieuwe Gentweg 5; tel: 050 33 07 75; www.quasimundo.com).

Canal Rides

There are several jetties for boat tours: behind the Church of our Lady (Onze-Lieve-Vrouwekerk), along the street the Dijver, beside the Fish Market (Vismarkt) and on Rozenhoedkaai. For information: Katelijnestraat 4; tel: 050 33 27 71; www.nvstael.com; Mar–Nov 10am–6pm. Boats sometimes operate out of season if the weather is good.

Horse-Drawn Carriages

The horse-drawn carriage tours depart from the Markt (Burg on Wed) and can carry 5 adults. The tour takes 35 minutes, including a drink-stop for the horse at the Beguinage, where passengers can get off and visit. See De Brugse Koetsiers, p/a Gemene Weidestraat 51; tel: 050 34 54 01; www.hippo.be/koets; daily 9.30am–5.30pm.

Bruges–Damme by Paddle-Steamer

The 'Lamme Goedzak' paddle-steamer moors at Noorweegse Kaai 31, just beyond Dampoort, and departs several times a day for Damme, 7km (4 miles) away, before making the return trip. The journey takes half an hour. See Damme Tourist Office; tel: 050 28 86 10; www.bootdamme-brugge.be; 1 Apr–15 Oct; five departures daily each way.

TRANSPORT

Airports and Arrival

The majority of international airlines fly into Brussels airport (tel: 0900 700 00, +32 27 53 77 53 (from abroad); www.brusselsairport.be) near Zaventem, 12km (7 miles) northeast of Brussels. A train station beneath the airport has direct services to Brussels and Ghent, from where connecting services take you to Bruges. The journey via Brussels or Ghent (both one change) takes 1 hour 30 mins. A taxi ride will cost around €250.

Low-cost airlines use Brussels South–Charleroi airport (www.charleroi-airport.com), 50km (30 miles) to the south. Coaches ferry passengers to and from Brussels in around 1 hour (see Voyages L'Elan; www.voyages-lelan.be).

Paris and Amsterdam airports are also within reach via high-speed train to Brussels, then inter-city train to Bruges.

By Sea

Cross-channel ferries from the UK serve seaports in easy reach of Bruges.
Dover–Calais: Only P&O Ferries (tel: 08716 642 121; www.poferries.com) now operates on this busy route, with several ferries daily. Crossings take 90 minutes. Calais is 120km (75 miles) from Bruges.
Dover–Dunkirk: Norfolkline schedules about 11 crossings daily each way, journey time 2 hours (tel: 0871 574 7235; www.norfolkline.com). Dunkirk is 76km (47 miles) from Bruges.
Ramsgate–Ostend: Transeuropa Ferries operate eight passenger crossings daily, taking 4 hours (tel: 01843

Above from far left: horse-drawn carriage; peaceful canal scene; bikes are a great way of touring the city.

7:31	KNOKKE		IC	8A
7:33	KORTRIJK		IC	7
7:34	BLANKENBERGE		IC	8B
7:35	BRUSSEL TONGEREN		IC	5
7:37	OOSTENDE		IC	6
7:37	GENT SINT-PIE...		L	2
7:54	OOSTENDE		P	10
7:57	ANTWERPEN ... L		IC	8
8:00	OOSTENDE		IC	10

595 522; www.transeuropaferries.co.uk). Ostend is 30km (18 miles) from Bruges.

Hull–Zeebrugge: P&O Ferries run a nightly service from Hull to Zeebrugge (every other night in January). Journey time around 12 hours.

By Rail

International trains from Paris, London and Amsterdam stop in Brussels. Eurostar services from London (St Pancras) and Kent (Ebbsfleet or Ashford) serve Brussels in under 2 hours, up to 10 times a day. Fares include free onward travel on Belgian railways to any Belgian station (within 24 hours of the arrival time stamped on the Eurostar ticket). See www.eurostar.com for reservations, or tel: 08705 186 186; outside UK, tel: +44 1233 617 575. There is a £5 charge for booking by phone.

Trains to Bruges run around twice an hour from Brussels, and take just under 1 hour. For timetables, see the Belgian railways (SNCB/NMBS) website (www.b-rail.be). Inter-city trains (IC) are comfortable, with toilets but no refreshments. They are often crowded at weekends and in the summer. The main station lies just outside the Old City. It takes about 10 minutes to walk into town; there are also frequent shuttle buses from the station to the Markt.

By Road

Bruges is located near the E40 motorway. The drive from Brussels takes just over 1 hour outside of peak times. Drivers from Britain can take the Eurotunnel from Folkestone to Calais, a drive-on, drive-off train service that takes 35 mins, or 1 hour from motorway to motorway. The service runs 24 hours a day, all year, with up to five departures an hour. Book in advance for best prices and to avoid a wait. Toll booths accept cash, cheques or credit cards. The price applies to the car, regardless of the number of passengers or car size. Eurotunnel (UK tel: 0990 353 535; www.eurotunnel.com). From Calais, allow 1 hour 20 mins to drive to Bruges (follow signs to Brugge Centrum).

Public Transport

Bus. As Bruges is so compact, you will rarely need to use the city buses, which are all operated by Flemish public transport company De Lijn. The central loop bus service (0/Centrum) links the rail station, 't Zand and the Markt. A single ticket bought on the bus costs €1.60 and is valid for 1 hour (including any change of bus within the Bruges zone). Day passes and 10-journey passes are also available and save money. Tickets must be entered in the scanner machine by the doors whenever you board a bus.

Taxis. In Bruges taxis can be recognised by the insignia on their roof. There are stands at the station and the Markt square.

Brugse Taxi: tel: 050 33 44 55
Rony's Taxis: tel: 050 34 43 44
Taxi Rita: tel: 050 35 30 73

Driving. Driving and parking within Bruges centre is not advised, as the old centre is a network of one-way streets. Tourists are advised to leave vehicles at the large car park next to the station (Stationsplein) or one of the other car parks in the city. Drop baggage at your hotel first. The charge for parking here is reasonable and includes free travel on the city buses. Claim a free ticket for each person in the car by showing your car park ticket at the De Lijn office outside the station.

Driving is on the right, with overtaking on the left. Vehicles coming from the right always have priority unless road markings indicate otherwise. Roads are generally safe, but speeding can be a problem. The blood alcohol limit for drivers is 0.5mg/litre (one glass of wine). Police have the power to carry out random alcohol tests.

Car Hire. The minimum age for car hire is 21 or 22 (some firms charge higher rates to those under 25). You need a passport, driving licence (valid for at least one year) and a credit card, on which a deposit is blocked until the vehicle is returned.
Budget: tel: 02 721 50 97; www.budget.be
Hertz: tel: 02 717 32 01; www.hertz.be
Avis: tel: 070 22 30 01; www.avis.be

V

VISAS AND PASSPORTS

EU nationals require only a valid personal identity card or passport to visit Belgium. Visitors from the US, Canada, Australia or New Zealand need a valid passport but not a visa if staying for less than three months.

Nationals of other countries may need a visa, costing around €60 (for a short-stay visa), which should be obtained from the embassy or consulate responsible for your place of residence before you travel. Apply 3–4 weeks prior to departure. Your passport must be valid for three months longer than the visa.

For more information (and if visiting for over 90 days), check www.diplomatie.be or with the Belgian embassy in your home country. Belgian law requires everyone over the age of 12 to carry an identity card or passport at all times.

W

WOMEN

Women in Belgium have equal rights, and it is safe for women to travel alone. In cities, dress conservatively if walking around at night and be aware of bag-snatchers and pickpockets; this is more of a problem in Brussels and Antwerp than in Bruges. Unwelcome approaches are best deterred by a firm but friendly response.

Above from far left: Bruges is well connected to the rest of Belgium by rail; local beer produced by the Half Moon Brewery (see p.48).

As a favourite destination for romantic getaways, Bruges is blessed with cosy hotels in medieval properties with canal views and period features. It presents more of a challenge to budget travellers or those looking for large rooms, a lift, gym or easy parking. Price deals vary and breakfast, if not included, is probably overpriced and worth seeking elsewhere. Be aware, too, that with canals may come a certain drainy whiff, and mosquitoes in warmer months. Pay for a view of the water if you wish, but in a city full of awesome views at every turn, you may decide this is a dispensable feature unless the hotel has air-conditioning. All the hotels bar one are in the historic centre, so walking to sights is not a problem. Bus routes from the station or 't Zand are also listed.

Centre

Crowne Plaza Brugge

Burg 10; tel: 050 44 68 44; www.crowneplaza.com/bruggebel; bus: 0/Centrum; €–€€€

It's hard to forgive the town planners who allowed this featureless edifice to be built on the historic Burg square. Inside, however, you get the fabulous view out,

Price for a double room for one night including breakfast:	
€€€€	over 200 euros
€€€	130–200 euros
€€	80–130 euros
€	below 80 euros

roomy bedrooms, big beds, swish bathrooms and the details and service you would expect from a top hotel, including kettles in rooms, a rare thing in Belgium. The basement contains the ruins of St Donatian's, the former cathedral, which makes for a bizarre feature in a conference suite. Underground parking is available beneath the hotel and low-season room rates can be excellent.

Martin's Orangerie

Kartuizerinnenstraat 10; tel: 050 34 16 49; www.martinshotels.com; bus: 0/Centrum; €€€€

Situated in a narrow street close to the Belfry, the Orangerie could not be more central. A former 15th-century convent, it is a romantic choice, with the water of the Dijver canal lapping at its terrace and just 20 rooms, all prettily furnished. A stylish makeover has transformed it into a cosy boutique hotel furnished with fine antiques, a wood-panelled dining room and a lounge like a private members' club. Try to avoid ground-floor rooms facing the street.

Relais Bourgondisch Cruyce

Wollestraat 41–47; tel: 050 33 79 26; www.relaisbourgondischcruyce. be; bus: 1, 11, 6, 16; €€€

A gorgeous small hotel in two gabled houses with timbered facades backing onto a canal. Decorated in sumptuous 17th-century Flemish style with carved furniture, stone floors and large fireplaces – if you've seen *In Bruges*, you'll

recognise it from the film. The 16 bed-rooms combine traditional decor with modern design. If you can, it is worth paying extra here for a canal-view room.

Walburg

Boomgaardstraat 13–15; tel: 050 34 94 14; www.hotelwalburg.be; bus: 6, 16; €€€

This spacious, elegant hotel occupies a restored historic mansion just 100m/yds from the Burg. All rooms have large, Italian marble bathrooms; high ceilings and elaborate cornices abound; rooms are larger than average, but suites are often in one large room rather than two. Breakfast includes cooked and conti-nental options and staff will happily recommend restaurants.

South

Boat-Hotel De Barge

Bargeweg 15; tel: 050 38 51 50; www.hoteldebarge.be; bus: 2, 12; €€€

Wake up to the sound of ducks outside the window in this unusual hotel located in a converted Flemish canal barge. The rooms (cabins) may be small, but they have an appealing nautical flavour, with white wood, blue paint and bright red lifejackets laid out on the beds. The hotel has a bar, terrace, restaurant and car park. Located just outside the Old Town, a brisk 10-minute walk from the centre beside a coach park (not visible) and conveniently near the railway sta-tion. At the low end of the price range.

Botaniek

Waalsestraat 23; tel: 050 34 14 24; www.botaniek.be; bus: 6, 16; €€

A homely little hotel with a warm wel-come, situated between the centre and Astrid Park in a quiet neighbourhood. The nine-room establishment occupies an 18th-century townhouse furnished in Louis XV style, fresh but without pre-tension. Rooms on the top floor have wonderful views of gabled houses and ancient spires. There is also a small lift, rare for a characterful hotel in Bruges.

Jan Brito

Freren Fonteinstraat 1; tel: 050 33 06 01; www.janbrito.eu; bus: 6, 16; €€–€€€

This 23-room hotel occupies a 16th-century merchant's house with a secluded Renaissance garden. Staff are friendly, and furnishings and decoration classic and tasteful. Room styles and prices vary enormously, from suites to the 'Maid's Room', a budget option!

't Keizershof

Oostmeers 126; tel: 050 33 87 28; www.hotelkeizershof.be; bus: 0/Centrum; €

The perfect place for anyone travelling on a tight budget, this compact, seven-room establishment is located close to the railway station and the Minnewater Park. The rooms are as cheap as they come, but are clean and comfortable. Each has a sink; shared toilets and shower rooms are on the landing.

Above from far left: Boat-Hotel De Barge; Die Swaene (see p.110).

Bed and Breakfast

There are a good number of bed and breakfast options in Bruges, many in tastefully renovated homes whose owners are keen to share their city's charms. Inexpensive compared to hotels, this option is worth considering if you don't require a mini-bar or room service, but book early as rooms are limited. Several B&B add-resses are listed at www.brugge-bed andbreakfast.com (a handy map graphic gives an instant location guide) or the Tourist Office site www. brugge.be, which has a more com-plete list. Bookings can normally be made online, but be aware that few owners accept credit cards.

Montanus

Nieuwe Gentweg 78; tel: 050 33 11 76; www.montanus.be; bus: 1, 11; €€€

This historic house was once the home of a Belgian statesmen; now it is the picture of restrained elegance, with rooms in muted natural tones either in the mansion or in the colonial-style pavilion in the garden, a 1920s former boarding school, where there is also a cedarwood honeymoon suite. Of the 20 rooms, one is suitable for disabled guests.

The Pand

Pandreitje 16; tel: 050 34 06 66; www.pandhotel.com; bus: 6, 16; €€€

This award-winning 23-room hotel is located near the prettiest view in Bruges centre, the famous Rozenhoedkaai. Formerly an 18th-century carriage house, it is now a boutique hotel brimming with style. Bedrooms are appealing, if on the small side. The breakfast room is furnished in country-house-kitchen style and breakfasts are famously good.

Die Swaene

Steenhouwersdijk 1; tel: 050 34 27 98; www.dieswaene.com; bus: 6, 16; €€€€

It's hard not to fall in love with this lovely hotel along a quiet, tree-lined canal close to the centre. It is in an irresistible building, with old wooden staircases and heavy oak furniture. The 22 rooms come in different sizes and styles, some of them replete with elegant four-poster beds, some – the downstairs rooms – on the dark and poky side. A candlelit restaurant, pool and sauna add to the allure and charm of the place. The hotel-owned Pergola Kaffee across the canal also has an enviable location.

De Tuilerieen

Dijver 7; tel: 050 34 36 91; www.hoteltuilerieen.com; bus: 0/Centrum; €€€€

The most luxurious hotel in town: a 45-room pale pink mansion facing the main canal. With courteous staff and a series of plush, antique-stuffed rooms, this is a hotel that is hard to resist returning to. Some rooms have views of the canal, while others face the garden; size can vary quite a bit, though, so check what you're getting. There is also a bright swimming pool and hammam.

West

Ensor

Speelmansrei 10; tel: 050 34 25 89; www.ensorhotel.be; bus: 0/Centrum; €–€€

This friendly 12-room hotel occupies a brick building on a quiet canal close to 't Zand. The rooms are plainly furnished but well-maintained, and some are quite large, with enough beds for up to four people. All have en-suite facilities with shower and WC, making this one of the best budget hotels in the city. If you have a vehicle, you can reserve a space in the private garage, but must do so in advance.

Karel De Stoute

Moerstraat 23; tel: 050 34 33 17;
www.hotelkareldestoute.be;
bus: 0/Centrum, 12; €–€€

Named after the 15th-century duke of Burgundy Charles the Bold, this intimate hotel occupies a building that once formed part of the Prinsenhof ducal residence, where Charles held his wedding feast. Run by a friendly couple, this nine-room establishment offers a relaxed atmosphere in the heart of the Old Town. The rooms vary but are mainly spacious and attractive. Some have oak beams, while two have bathrooms located in a 15th-century circular staircase tower. There is an attractive cellar bar with a vaulted ceiling, and internet access is free. If you want to avoid steep stairs, ask for a lower floor.

Kempinski Hotel Dukes' Palace

Prinsenhof 8; tel: 050 44 78 88;
www.kempinski.com/bruges;
bus: 0/Centrum; €€€€

An exclusive choice occupying the neo-Gothic Prinsenhof, a 19th-century rebuild of the medieval Princes' Court created by Burgundian Duke Philip the Good in 1429. Following a major renovation in 2008 under new ownership (luxury hotel group Kempinski), it now boasts 21st-century standards of luxury (pool, banqueting facilities, car park) and bags of historic cachet.

Prinsenhof

Ontvangersstraat 9; tel: 050 34 26 90; www.prinsenhof.be; bus: 0/Centrum; €€€

Not to be confused with the Dukes' Palace in the former Prinsenhof, this elegant hotel is traditionally furnished, with wood panelling, chandeliers and other antiques; it has comfortable beds and excellent bathrooms. There is a warm atmosphere, and the staff will go out of their way to ensure your stay is memorable. The 16 rooms are often reserved well in advance, so book early.

Snuffel Sleep-In

Ezelstraat 47–49; tel: 050 33 31 33;
www.snuffel.be; bus: 3, 13; €

A simple youth hostel with pine bunks in rooms sleeping four to 12 people (the small rooms can also be booked as private rooms for two people – in which case go for the en-suite option). Located in a traditional gabled house, it has a ground-floor bar with English newspapers, internet access, its own beer and live gigs every first and third Saturday of the month, except July and August. Beer and breakfast are cheap, and the atmosphere is perfect for young people.

Price for a double room for one night including breakfast:

€€€€	over 200 euros
€€€	130–200 euros
€€	80–130 euros
€	below 80 euros

Above from far left: grandly styled breakfast room at Jan Brito (see p.109); four poster at The Pand.

Asiris

Lange Raamstraat 9; tel: 050 34 17 24; www.hotelasiris.be; bus: 4, 14; €

A small, family-run hotel in a quiet quarter close to St Giles' Church (Sint-Gilliskerk). The 11 bedrooms are furnished in a plain, modern style aimed at families and travellers on a budget. Breakfast is included in the price, making this one of the best inexpensive hotels in town. Special rates are offered out of season.

Ter Brughe

Oost-Gistelhof 2; tel: 050 34 03 24; www.hotelterbrughe.com; bus: 4, 14; €€

This attractive hotel in the elegant St Giles quarter, 5 minutes from the centre of Bruges, has wood panelling and traditional charm, along with comfy beds. Breakfast is served in the 14th-century beamed and vaulted cellar, which was once a warehouse for goods brought along the canal. The 24 rooms are comfortable, if with a rather faded decor. Pay extra for a canal view: it's worth it.

Bryghia

Oosterlingenplein 4; tel: 050 33 80 59; www.bryghiahotel.be; bus: 4, 14; €€

This family-run hotel is situated in one of Bruges's most peaceful neighbourhoods, rarely visited by tourists but still very central. The 18-room hotel is in a 15th-century building once owned by Hanseatic merchants. The interior is cosy and tastefully furnished, with comfortable sofas and exposed wood beams, offering good value for the price. Some rooms enjoy a view of a sleepy canal.

Cavalier

Kuipersstraat 25; tel: 050 33 02 07; www.hotelcavalier.be; bus: 0/Centrum; €

In spite of its slightly ramshackle external appearance, this small hotel is friendly and ordered and provides good value for the cheaper range of hotels; it is also very central. The eight rooms are larger than average for Bruges and the breakfast is better than you might expect from the class of hotel. The stairs are steep, though, so if you have heavy luggage ask for a lower room.

Ter Duinen

Langerei 52; tel: 050 33 04 37; www.hotelterduinen.eu; bus: 4, 14; €€–€€€

A little out of the centre – read, nicely away from the crowds – 'The Dunes' takes its name from the former abbey across the canal. The owners have a stylish aesthetic and pay great attention to detail: the conservatory and formal garden are beautiful, and the rooms neutrally decorated and pleasant, many with laminate flooring. The cobbled Langerei can be busy in the day, but is quiet at night and windows are super-insulated. Air-conditioning in all rooms is a definite plus in warm

weather, as it gets around the mosqui-toes-versus-stuffiness dilemma that plagues many canalside properties.

Relais Oud-Huis Amsterdam

Genthof 4a; tel: 050 34 18 10; www.martins-hotels.com; bus: 4, 14; €€€

Overlooking a canal in the heart of the old Merchants' Quarter, this romantic 22-room hotel, set in a 17th-century trading house, has a wooden staircase, beams and stunning antique furniture. There is also a pretty interior courtyard. Skip the hotel breakfast, which costs extra, and walk 5 minutes to Het Dagelijks Brood (Philipstockstraat 21) to enjoy coffee and croissants in a typical French farmhouse interior.

East

Adornes

St Annarei 26; tel: 050 34 13 36; www.adornes.be; bus: 4, 14; €€

This pretty 20-room hotel occupies a row of traditional brick houses facing a canal in the charming St Anna quarter. The rooms are comfortable and bright, some with oak beams; decor is traditional verging on the dated. Breakfast is included in the price of the room and there are free bikes for guests' use, as well as a limited number of underground parking spaces.

Ter Reien

Langestraat 1; tel: 050 34 91 00; www.hotelterreien.be; bus: 6, 16; €€

'The Canals' hotel is an inexpensive option on the junction of two lovely canals, and occupies the house where the Symbolist painter Fernand Khnopff spent his childhood. All 26 rooms are non-smoking and are bright and comfortable, although some have rather-too-tiny bathrooms. They face the canal, courtyard or street, and prices reflect this. Breakfast can be taken in the pretty courtyard.

Out of Town

Leonardo

Chartreuseweg 20; tel: 050 40 21 40; www.leonardo-hotels.com; bus: 7, 74; €€

This out-of-town option between the motorway and the centre has had a stylish recent makeover and offers modern amenities, including an out-door pool with children's play area and easy parking, making it ideal for families. Most people will not want to stay this far from the centre, but a hired bike to cover the 5km (3 miles) from here to town is a good alternative to driving, a (pricey) taxi or the local bus – remember, Flanders is dead flat and all roads have good bike paths.

Above from far left: Martin's Orangerie *(see p.108)* occupies a lovely spot by the water; courtyard at The Pand boutique hotel *(see p.110)*.

Price for a double room for one night including breakfast:

€€€€	over 200 euros
€€€	130–200 euros
€€	80–130 euros
€	below 80 euros

Bruges has a long tradition of fine feasting and banqueting, a reputation its 21st-century inhabitants uphold in style. The West Flemish appreciate fresh seafood, grilled meats and the produce of the fertile interior: asparagus, endives, mushrooms and pungent Ardennes cheeses. But good food does not come cheap in a city centre thronging with tourists: avoid eating on the Markt square; consider eating a main meal at lunchtime when the best offers are available; and check the recommendations below – and in the Food and Drink listings in each walk chapter – for where to find a tasty meal at a fair price. Lunchtime is generally noon–2pm and dinner 7–9pm: the city shuts down early and few places are open late. Finally, it is wise to book ahead for an evening meal, even in the low season, as popular places are often booked out.

Centre

Breydel – De Coninck

Breidelsstraat 24; tel: 050 33 97 46; Thur–Tue noon–2pm, 6–10pm; €€
Unremarkable from the outside, but those in the know will tell you that this

Price guide for a two-course meal for one, with glass of house wine:

€€€€	over 100 euros
€€€	60–100 euros
€€	30–60 euros
€	below 30 euros

unpretentious dining room – named after the city's famed freedom fighters and a family business for over 50 years – is the go-to address for mussels (when in season; expect a large portion), lobster and eels. Street-view tables make it possible to while away an afternoon watching tourists being trotted around in carriages.

Chez Olivier

Meestraat 9; tel: 050 33 36 59; Mon–Wed, Fri noon–1.30pm, 7–9.30pm, Sat 7–9.30pm; €€€
This impeccable all-white dining room overlooks the most romantic stretch of canal in Bruges, from the corner of the Meebrug. It's a peaceful and upmarket choice, with only 10 tables and set in a beautiful 16th-century building. The cuisine is refined French-Belgian, with a focus on meat. Request a table overlooking the canal.

Duc de Bourgogne

Huidenvettersplein 12; tel: 050 33 20 38; www.ducdebourgogne.be; Tue 7–9.30pm, Wed–Sun noon–2.30pm, 7–9.30pm; €€€
On a touristy street, this hotel restaurant offers old-school dining, with French-style dishes in beautiful surroundings and a view over the most photographed canal scene in town. Sup like a lord on lobster and roast meat in rich sauce among the artworks and tapestries. The fixed-price menus are good value, especially for lunch.

Erasmus

Wollestraat 35; tel: 050 33 57 81;
www.hotelerasmus.com; Fri–Wed
noon–3pm, 6–10pm; €€

This sleek, grey-hued restaurant in the
eponymous hotel is a tippler's dream,
with a wide choice of beers to accom-
pany the beer-inspired dishes: try crown
of lamb with parsley and mustard,
served with potato and bacon gratin
made with Bush blond beer. A fair bit
cheaper than nearby beer-focused eatery
Den Dyver, but a bit less adventurous
too. The menu changes monthly.

Au Petit Grand

Philipstockstraat 18; tel: 050 34 86
71; www.aupetitgrand.be; Tue–Sun
6pm–midnight; €€

Fuel up on T-bone steak or rack of lamb
at this pretty and popular address near
the Burg,where the speciality is fish and
meat cooked on the grill, a Flemish
favourite. It is compact and the locals
like it here: if you're hoping for an intimate tête-à-tête, be aware that it can get
crowded and so may not be the place for
you. Advance reservation is advised.

De Stove

Kleine Sint-Amandsstraat 4; tel: 050
33 78 35; www.restaurantdestove.be;
Sat–Tue noon–1.30pm, 7–9.30pm,
Fri 7–9.30pm, closed two weeks in
Jan, two weeks in June; €€€

Homely and rustic De Stove specialises
in Flemish cuisine with an emphasis on
creative ways with salad, fish and steaks.

Try scallops on black pasta with tomato
tapenade; sea bream with couscous; or
stuffed aubergine and basil oil. The intimate 20-seater is unfussy, and set in an
old gabled house on a pedestrianised
street near the Markt. Prices are at the
lower end of this bracket.

De Visscherie

Vismarkt 8; tel: 050 33 02 12;
www.visscherie.be; Wed–Mon
noon–2pm, 7–10pm; €€€

The subtle flavours of the sea are cooked
to perfection at this top-notch fish and
seafood restaurant, situated right on the
Fish Market (Vismarkt). A formal
establishment where the maître d' will
attend to your every whim, this is ideal
for a special occasion with all the frills.
A few meat dishes are also available.

South

De Bron

Katelijnestraat 82; tel: 050 33 45 26;
www.eethuisdebron.be; Tue–Sat
11.45am–2pm; €

A guaranteed healthy and wholesome
option, this lunch-only vegetarian
restaurant is spotless and bright, with
an atrium at the rear. You join a table
wherever there is a seat and eat the
soup or dish of the day: a mixed platter
that might include a gratin, a grain and
baked, steamed and raw vegetables (just
choose which size dish you want; vegan
option on request). You have to ring the
bell to get in, but once in, the staff are
friendly and helpful.

**Above from far
left:** Erasmus;
classic Belgian dish
of mussels and
chips; De Stove.

Couvert

Eekhoutstraat 17; tel: 050 33 37 87;
www.couvert-brugge.be; Thur–Mon
noon–2pm, 6–10pm; €€
A loving attention to its French-style
cuisine, service and presentation have
earned this slightly backstreet address
a deservedly faithful following. The
fixed-price menu is inventive and seasonal – gratin of scallops and asparagus;
baked guinea fowl with stuffed mushrooms and creamy parsley sauce – while
the à la carte is brief but diverse. White-
dressed tables and brick-exposed walls
complete the setting for an intimate,
romantic experience.

Den Dyver

Dijver 5; tel: 050 33 60 69; www.
dyver.be; Fri–Tue noon–2pm, 6.30–
9.30pm, Thur 6.30–9.30pm; €€€
Embark on an adventure in taste at this
family-run house renowned for inventive beer cuisine. Think guinea fowl
and mint mousse in a Chimay sauce
with caramelised figs; spicy rabbit
roulade with prune and Rodenbach
chutney; or classic *bouillabaisse* (fish
stew) cooked with beer. All dishes
come with a recommendation for
accompanying Belgian beer, while
desserts are prepared with genever
(Belgian gin). Not cheap, but unique.

't Pandreitje

Pandreitje 6; tel: 050 33 11 90;
www.pandreitje.be; Mon, Tue, Fri,
Sat noon–1.30pm, 7–9pm; €€€

Elegant and refined Franco-Belgian
cuisine is served in spacious comfort in
this Renaissance-era patrician house
near the Rozenhoedkaai. Chef Guy Van
Neste runs the kitchen and wine cellar,
while his English-born wife welcomes
guests. The atmosphere is formal, in a
manner befitting the gastronomic
dishes, which may include baked sea
bass on a creamy watercress sauce with
artichokes, or roasted sweetbreads with
baby leeks and black truffles.

De Stoepa

Oostmeers 124; tel: 050 33 04 54;
www.stoepa.be; Tue–Sat 11.45am–
late, Sun from 1pm; €
This fusion bar-restaurant near the
station is popular for its informal atmosphere and exotic cuisine, not to mention
a walled back garden, which is a fantastic sun trap on fine days. When the
trendy staff aren't too busy being too
cool (or rude) to serve you, the menu is
varied and vegetarian-friendly – wok
dishes, curries, salads, and many nibbles with dips – but locals come here as
much for a cheerful night out with
friends as a serious tuck-in. The kitchen
is open noon–2pm and 6pm–midnight.

Tanuki

Oude Gentweg 1; tel: 050 34 75 12;
www.tanuki.be; Wed–Sun noon–
2pm, 6.30–9.30pm, closed mid-July,
school holiday in Feb and around 1
Nov; €€€
Step off Katelijnestraat and enter a

Above from far left: Den Dyver; Belgian waffles; cockles from the Fish Market.

calm Japanese interior where the rules of Zen harmony predominate and presentation is tip-top. Sushi, sashimi and teppanyaki are prepared at one end of the dining room in an open kitchen, while in winter the menu is boosted with the addition of warming options like Suki-yaki and Shabu-shabu (two varieties of meat hotpot) and Yosenabe (chicken, seafood and vegetable casserole). Prices reflect the cost of the super-fresh fish and skilled chefs required for the perfect sushi.

't Zwaantje

Gentpoortvest 70; tel: 04 73 71 25 80; www.hetzwaantje.be; Fri–Tue noon–2pm, 6.30–10pm; €€
Belgian-French cuisine is lovingly presented and served at this local treasure that tourists have never really discovered, partly because it is on the perimeter canal far from most attractions (off Katelijnestraat). Tiffany-style lamps, mirrors and candlelight will fulfill all your romantic fantasies while the welcome is homely and warm, a far cry from some of the tourist traps elsewhere. As well as good steaks, stew and skate, the chef has won prizes for his chocolate desserts. You have been warned...

West

Aneth

Marie van Bourgondiëlaan 1; tel: 050 31 11 89; www.aneth.be; Tue–Fri and 2nd Sun of month, noon–2pm, 7–9pm, Sat 7–9pm; €€€€

Local foodies who like their fish adore Aneth and book ahead to celebrate special occasions with its dazzling cuisine. Set in a roomy, detached house beside the Graaf Visartpark outside the ring road to the west, this place is well off the tourist circuit, but you will not regret the trip if you fancy a gastronomic preparation of the day's catch. The chef's speciality is the use of herbs preserved in alcohol, as well as other weird and wonderful accompaniments. True artistry on a plate.

Chagall

Sint-Amandsstraat 40; tel: 050 33 61 12; Thur–Tue 11am–11.30pm; €
Whether you are out for a few drinks or for a heart-warming pot of mussels in cream sauce, you may have to fight for a table on this popular bistro's terrace, which is perfect for people-watching and afternoon sun on the pedestrianised Sint-Amandsstraat. Classical music plays in the cosy interior, which has an open hearth, wooden beams and stained-glass windows. Very good value for good quality in a central location.

Price guide for a two-course meal for one, with glass of house wine:

€€€€	over 100 euros
€€€	60–100 euros
€€	30–60 euros
€	below 30 euros

Grand Café De Passage

Dweersstraat 26; tel: 050 34 02 32;
www.passagebruges.com; bar
5pm–midnight and later, kitchen
6–11pm; €

A surprisingly good cheap-eat in an overpriced town: this long brown café in *belle époque* style is packed with tables. Locals love it and, thanks to the hostel upstairs (rather less well reputed than the café), a lively atmosphere is guaranteed. Good for ribs and grilled food, served with jacket potatoes or chips.

Guillaume

Korte Lane 20; tel: 050 34 46 05;
www.guillaume2000.be; Wed–Sun
D only; €€€

A traditional whitewashed cottage on a terraced street north of 't Zand houses a high-quality bistro run by owner-chef Wim Vansteelant, famous for its 'after party' once the plates are cleared. The menu includes a small but tasty selection of starters and main courses with a distinct Franco-Belgian flavour, such as mackerel stuffed with Liège potatoes and mustard ham.

De Mangerie

Oude Burg 20; tel: 050 33 93 36;
www.mangerie.com; Tue–Sat
noon–1.30pm, 7–9.30pm; €€€

The young couple who run this restaurant have gained a reputation for their scrummy dishes and superb presentation – and a short menu fea-

turing a starter and main course from each of four styles: modern Belgian, Mediterranean, Eastern and vegetarian; dishes include the likes of scallops with creamed aubergines, confit tomatoes and basil, and veal sweetbreads with Belgian asparagus and vintage sherry.

North

Brasserie Souffleur

Vlamingstraat 58; tel: 050 34 82 92;
www.souffleur.be; Fri–Wed 11am–
11pm; €€

This brisk and smart brasserie across the road from the city theatre is renowned for copious and original salads, but also meat and fish dishes, including good mussels and chips. There is a warming open hearth in winter and a sunny terrace streetside in summer. Popular with ladies who lunch and other locals; there is usually ample space at lunchtime, but booking is advised in the evening.

Kok au Vin

Ezelstraat 21; tel: 050 33 95 21;
www.kok-au-vin.be; Tue–Sat
11.45–2pm, 18.30–10pm; €€

This friendly restaurant serves up excellent Belgian fare in a chic setting. Yet for all of its traditional dishes and warm décor, the food is deceptively sophisticated. North sea fish, local veal and steak tartare all impress, but the eponymous coq-au-vin steals the show.

Zeno

Vlamingstraat 53; tel: 050 68 09 93;
www.restaurantzeno.be; Tue–Fri
noon–2pm, 7–9pm, Sat 7–9pm; €€
Named after an alchemist in a Mar-
guerite Yourcenar novel, this restaurant
is run by a young couple who are passionate about sourcing the best
ingredients and combining them in a
magical way. Their one-monthly menu
is composed of eight courses from which
you select four to seven dishes, or else a
faster lunch option. The Franco-Belgian
cuisine is excellent, but if you loathe
nouvelle cuisine this place is not for you.

East

Bistro Refter

Molenmeers 2; tel: 050 44 49 00;
Tue–Sat L and D; €€–€€€
A new venture of Geert Van Hecke (*see*
De Karmeliet), this upmarket brasserie
(*refter*, refectory) opened in 2009 and
brings his culinary magic within the
reach of mere mortals, while sparing
them the pomp and ceremony of his
landmark restaurant. Dishes are vari-
ations on the bistro standards: asparagus
served every which way; snails, fish
soup, scallops, and so on. The wine list
is good and seating comfortable if not
spacious. Reserve well in advance.

De Karmeliet

Langestraat 19; tel: 050 33 82 59;
www.dekarmeliet.be; Tue–Sat
noon–3pm, 6–11pm, plus Easter
and Whit Sunday; €€€€

A legend beyond Belgium's borders, De
Karmeliet occupies a gastronomic class
of its own, created by indefatigable
owner-chef Geert Van Hecke. Defending the three Michelin stars he's held for
12 years, he draws on Belgian specialities – North Sea fish, hop shoots, endive
and asparagus. The patrician mansion
has a comfortable lounge and formal
dining rooms, but service can be a little
stiff. Count around €150 a head
depending on menu and wine choice.

Rock Fort

Langestraat 15; tel: 050 33 41 13;
www.rock-fort.be; Mon–Fri 12.30–
2pm, 6.30–11pm; €€–€€€
Langestraat has become something of
a gastro mecca in recent years, with
new planets orbiting De Karmeliet's
star. It has gained a name for fantastic
food in a stylish but unstuffy setting.
The chef has a strong background in
French cuisine and injects other world
influences to thrilling effect, such as
noodle soup with gambas, pig cheeks
in Arrabiata sauce, or veal haunch in
whisky. It's not a large space, so be sure
to book in advance.

**Above from far
left:** Zeno court-
yard and dessert;
Bistro Refter.

Price guide for a two-course
meal for one, with glass of
house wine:

€€€€	over 100 euros
€€€	60–100 euros
€€	30–60 euros
€	below 30 euros

As a small city with no university bar the elite postgrad College of Europe, the best nightlife in Bruges tends to be of the well-behaved variety: excellent classical music, contemporary dance and the odd jazz or rock gig, or quiet bars ideal for a drink among friends. If you want a thumping club, head for Ghent, Antwerp or Kortrijk: some bars have dance floors and are free, but these tend to appeal mainly to the very young. This chapter highlights the main cultural venues and a selection of bars for aperitifs or late evening drinks, including a few for dancing. It also picks some of the many festivals that Bruges puts on throughout the year, which may determine when you choose to visit.

Music, Theatre and Dance

Concert Hall

't Zand 34; tel: 050 47 69 99; box office: 070 22 33 02; www.concert gebouw.be

The modern Concert Hall (Concertge- bouw) has been credited with helping the city prove that it is more than a living museum, buried in the past. It has a rep- utation for highbrow programming, with an emphasis on authentic music, performed as the composer intended. Period instrument symphony orchestra Anima Eterna, led by harpsichordist Jos van Immerseel, has been in residence since the building opened in 2002, but contemporary classical and electronica also feature. Touring ballet, modern dance and opera productions also play

here. It holds an annual dance festival in December and co-produces the biennial Jazz Brugge with De Werf *(see below)*.

Cultuurcentrum Brugge/ City Theatre

Vlamingstraat 29; tel: 050 44 30 40; box office: 050 44 30 60; www. cultuurcentrumbrugge.be

The neoclassical City Theatre (Stads- schouwburg) is the core venue of Cultuurcentrum Brugge, a network of performance spaces across the city which is anything but classical in its pro- gramming. Dance, live music (rock, pop, world and folk) and theatre form the mainstay, but visual art exhibitions also feature. Other venues include a 17th- century former chapel, the Hallen com- plex beneath the Belfort, and the MaZ, used by the Cactus Club *(see opposite)*.

De Werf

Werfstraat 108; tel: 050 33 05 29; www.dewerf.be

This theatre, jazz and blues venue has its own record label. Visiting artists come from all over the world, and there are monthly free jam sessions. Best known for its close association with Bruges- born jazz pianist and composer Kris Defoort, it is the motor behind the Jazz Brugge festival, which focuses on cur- rent trends in European jazz and is held biannually over one week in September (next held in 2010). Theatre productions include contemporary new works and children's and young people's theatre.

NIGHTLIFE

Cactus Musiekcentrum

MaZ, Magdalenastraat 27, 8200 Brugge Sint-Andries; tel: 050 71 68 40; www.cactusmusic.be

Cactus is the city's principal rock, world and alternative concert promoter, whose main venue is the Cactus Club@MaZ (Magdalenazaal). It puts on an eclectic concert schedule featuring major international names in rock, pop, country, electronica and experimental, as well as local young bands. In early July, it holds the three-day Cactus Festival in the Minnewater Park *(see Festivals, p.123)*.

(see Festivals, p.123)

Film

Cinema Liberty

Kuipersstraat 23; tel: 050 33 20 11; www.cinema-liberty.be

A decent cinema in the centre of Bruges, just behind the City Theatre, with a range of arthouse and mainstream films.

Lumière

Sint-Jacobsstraat 36; tel: 050 34 34 65; www.lumiere.be

With three screens, this central venue shows arthouse and mainstream films. It is attached to the De Republiek café.

Nightlife

Barsalon

Langestraat 15; tel: 050 33 41 13; www.rock-fort.be; Mon–Fri noon–2.30pm, 5pm–1am (2am Fri); free

This trendy lounge bar-bistro occupies a sliver of a place next to Rock Fort restaurant *(see p.119)*; it belongs to the same team and serves smart food to match. Ideal for a tête-à-tête.

(see p.119)

B-In

Zonnekemeers – Oud Sint-Jan; tel: 050 31 13 00; www.b-in.be; Tue–Sat 11am–2am; free

This designer lounge bar in the area behind Memling in Sint-Jan Museum has live DJ sets every Fri and Sat night, but can be soulless when quiet. The waterside terrace is a pleasant spot for early evening drinks, though.

't Brugs Beertje

Kemelstraat 5; tel: 050 33 96 16; www.brugsbeertje.be; Thur–Tue 4pm–1am, Sat–Sun until 2am; free

The beer connoisseur's favourite bar in Bruges, as small inside as its reputation is large, this has become something of a mecca since it was established some 20 years ago, thanks to the knowledgeable landlord who can advise on all aspects of his 300 or so beers. Snacks and light meals are served, and there is a shop on-site where you can buy the T-shirt.

Cambrinus

Philipstockstraat 19; tel: 050 33 23 28; www.cambrinus.eu; daily 11am–11pm, later Sat–Sun; free

Under the same ownership as nearby beer store De Bier Tempel, this brasserie has similar expertise in the hallowed hop: 400 beers are on offer in a renovated pub-like decor with coloured glass

Above from far left: for a vast range of beers, try Cambrinus; packed bar.

lamps, a long bar and table service. It also serves good portions of hearty food – including recipes cooked with beer.

Het Entrepot

Binnenweg 4; tel: 050 47 07 80; www.hetentrepot.be; regular parties and gigs from 8 or 9pm–4am; charge

This old customs building just outside the ring canal, north of the city, hosts everything from club nights and gigs to dance classes and jam sessions. Check website or flyers and posters around town for details of parties.

La Fuente

Vrijdagmarkt 15; tel: 0478 20 33 07; Mon, Thur, Fri 3pm–3am; Sat 10am–4am; Sun 4pm–4am; free

An attractive bar on the west side of 't Zand square, La Fuente is run by a young couple, and popular with a slightly older crowd who just want to let loose to chart-toppers and dance-floor classics from the 70s and 80s. It's a pleasant place for either a pleasant aperitif or a late drink and a boogie.

Joey's Café

Zilverpand; tel: 050 34 12 64; Mon–Sat 11.30am–2am, 3am or 4am; free

Jazzy sounds play late into the night at this small café (with an outdoor terrace) in the Zilverpand shopping centre. Run by a friendly local musician, this is a relaxed place to enjoy good music long after most of Bruges has gone to bed.

De Lokkedize

Korte Vulderstraat 33; tel: 050 33 44 50; www.lokkedize.be; Wed–Sun from 6pm, Fri–Sat until 1am; free

A favourite, this convivial café is run by a friendly couple. The well-priced food in a candlelit setting is followed at weekends by live bands playing a variety of R&B, jazz, folk and rock. Popular with locals and often very busy, you can still show up pretty late and still get the lovely home-cooked food.

Du Phare

Sasplein 2; tel: 050 34 35 90; www. duphare.be; Wed–Mon 11.30am–1am, Sat–Sun until 4am; food served: 12.30–3pm, 6pm–midnight; free

Up near the Dampoort at the end of Langerei, this music bar-brasserie has a friendly atmosphere, a varied menu (Creole, Thai, steaks) and once a month a live concert with a blues or jazz band. A large south-facing terrace beside the canal is a draw on sunny days, but after dark is its busiest time.

Retsin's Lucifernum

Twijnstraat 6–8; tel: 0476 35 06 51; Sat 9pm–2am; Sun 6pm–10pm; charge

This old Bruges townhouse is opened once a week by its owner, the eccentric artist Willy Retsin. This former Masonic lodge is packed with paintings, sculptures and curios; the bar serves rum cocktails (only), and the music is Latin American and gypsy, sometimes live.

Wereldcafé De Republiek

Sint-Jacobsstraat 36; tel: 050 34 02 29; www.derepubliek.be; daily 11am–late; free

A bohemian crowd comes here to discuss politics, culture and the film they have just seen at the adjacent arthouse cinema. It is also a good place to pick up flyers about parties and other events.

Wijnbar Est

Braambergstraat 7; tel: 050 33 38 39; www.wijnbarest.be; Wed–Mon 4pm–midnight; free

A lovely shabby-chic wine bar whose female owner is passionate and knowledgeable. The daily menu of wines by the glass is chalked up on the blackboard; 90 other types are available by the bottle. Food includes platters of cheese and charcuterie, salad and pasta, all designed to enhance the tasting experience. There are intimate live concerts every Sunday from 8–10.30pm, and the music might be jazz, blues, boogie, folk or pop; entry is free.

Festivals

Holy Blood Procession

Ascension Day; www.holyblood.com

A religious procession held every year on Ascension Day (May), in which biblical scenes are re-enacted and the relic of the Holy Blood is paraded through the city by the bishop, followed by a retinue of local people dressed as crusaders and knights. A long-established event on the Catholic Church calendar – a

procession was first recorded in 1291 – you'll need to purchase tickets for seats along the route well in advance.

Cactus Festival

Early July; www.cactusfestival.be

This small-scale rock and world music festival in the Minnewater Park is adorable for its village-fete atmosphere.

Reiefeest

Third week in Aug, every three years; www.reiefeest.be

The canal festival of theatre, pageantry, dancing and light shows is held every three years (next scheduled for 2014), involves hundreds of performers and thousands of spectators. Book a ticket to enter the central area and follow the action on the water and in the Burg.

Pageant of the Golden Tree

Late Aug, every five years; www.comitevoorinitiatief.be

Recreating a medieval festival (Praalstoet van de Gouden Boom) staged to celebrate the marriage of Charles the Bold, duke of Burgundy, and Margaret of York, this costumed pageant (next scheduled for 2017) drew 100,000 spectators in 2007.

Snow and Ice Bruges

Nov–Jan; www.icesculpture.be

This ice sculpture attraction is a winter highlight: ice-artists from across northern Europe craft ice models on a designated theme.

Above from far left: live music at Het Entrepot; Pageant of the Golden Tree.

CREDITS

Insight Step by Step Bruges
Written by: Katharine Mill
Updated by: Nicholas Hirst
Series Editor: Carine Tracanelli
Cartography Editors: Zoë Goodwin
and James Macdonald
Map Production: Stephen Ramsay and
Phoenix Mapping
Picture Manager: Yoshimi Kanazawa
Art Editor: Richard Cooke
Photography: All pictures © APA/Glyn Genin,
except APA/Chris Coe 7MR; APA/Jerry Dennis
6BR, 60TR, 64B, 64T, 66TL, 71, 75T, 77TL;
APA/Georgie Scott 7CL, 82/83, 83TR, 84TL,
85TR, 87T, 92B, 93TR; APA Gregory Wrona
2BR, 6T, 17TR, 72TL, 82TL, 88B, 88C, 88T,
89T, 90T, 91T; Alamy 22T, 23T, 80T; Bruges
Tourism 7BL, 10T, 13TR, 28TL, 30TL, 34, 34T,
38B, 42T, 45TR, 50/51, 55/56, 57TL, 62T, 65T,
70, 97T, 104/105; Flanders Tourism 4T, 6MR/
ML; Fotolia 38T, 94BL; Getty 24/25, 69T
iStockphoto 11T, 12/13, 19, 51TR, 63T, 77TR,
86T; Daniël de Kievith 2/3; Leonardo 109T,
110T, 111T, 112T, 113T; Photolibrary 81T; Rex
Features 79T; Sophie van Passchaen 8BL; TIPS
100T 123T
Front cover: all 4Corners Images.

Printed by: CTPS – China

Second Edition 2012

Although Insight Guides and the authors of this
book have taken all reasonable care in preparing it,
we make no warranty about the accuracy or com-
pleteness of its content, and, to the maximum extent
permitted, disclaim all liability arising from its use.

CONTACTING THE EDITORS

We would appreciate it if readers would alert us
to errors or outdated information by writing to
us at insight@apaguide.co.uk or APA Publications,
PO Box 7910, London SE1 1WE, UK.

www.insightguides.com

DISTRIBUTION

Worldwide
APA Publications GmbH & Co. Verlag KG
(Singapore branch)
7030 Ang Mo Kio Ave 5
08-65 Northstar @ AMK, Singapore 569880
Email: apasin@singnet.com.sg

UK and Ireland
Dorling Kindersley Ltd
(a Penguin Company)
80 Strand, London, WC2R 0RL, UK
Email: customerservice@uk.dk.com

US
Ingram Publisher Services
One Ingram Blvd, PO Box 3006
La Vergne, TN 37086-1986
Email: customer.service@ingrampublisher
services.com

Australia
Universal Publishers
PO Box 307
St. Leonards NSW 1590
Email: sales@universalpublishers.com.au

New Zealand
Brown Knows Publications
11 Artesia Close, Shamrock Park
Auckland, New Zealand 2016
Email: sales@brownknows.co.nz

INDEX